Numerology
DECODER

Numerology DECODER

UNLOCK THE POWER OF NUMBERS TO REVEAL YOUR INNERMOST DESIRES
AND FORETELL YOUR FUTURE

RICHARD CRAZE

A QUARTO BOOK

Copyright © 2001 Quarto Inc.

First edition for the United States and
Canada published in 2001 by Barron's
Educational Series, Inc.

All inquiries should be addressed to:
Barron's Educational Series, Inc.
250 Wireless Boulevard
Hauppauge, NY 11788
http://www.barronseduc.com

International Standard Book No.
0-7641-1597-9

Library of Congress Catalog Card No.
00-104125

QUAR.1234

Conceived, designed and produced by
Quarto Publishing plc
The Old Brewery
6 Blundell Street
London N7 9BH

Editor   Steffanie Diamond Brown
Art editor   Elizabeth Healey
Copy editor   Rica Dearman
Designer   Tania Field
Photographer   Martin Norris
Illustrators   Tania Field, Matthew Cooper
Picture research   Laurent Boubounelle
Proofreader   Neil Cole
Indexer   Dorothy Frame

Art Director   Moira Clinch
Publisher   Piers Spence

Manufactured by Regent Publishing
Services Ltd, Hong Kong
Printed by Leefung-Asco Printers Ltd,
China
9 8 7 6 5 4 3 2 1

Contents

Introduction

FROM THE MOMENT YOU ARE BORN, YOU ARE ALLOCATED NUMBERS THAT ARE IMPORTANT TO YOU: YOUR DATE OF BIRTH, PASSPORT NUMBER, HOUSE NUMBER, SOCIAL SECURITY NUMBER, BANK ACCOUNT NUMBER, AND CAR LICENSE NUMBER, TO NAME BUT A FEW. SHOULD YOU EVER BE CONVICTED OF A FELONY, YOU'LL BE REDUCED TO THE MOST BASIC COMPONENT—THE PRISONER NUMBER. IN THIS BOOK, YOU WILL LEARN A GREAT DEAL ABOUT THE MAGIC OF NUMBERS, INCLUDING THEIR SYMBOLIC SIGNIFICANCE, THE NATURE OF THEIR VIBRATIONS, THEIR LORE, AND THEIR SECRET MEANINGS.

The history
of numerology

The letters of the Hebrew alphabet are based on numbers. According to the Kabbalists, the Scriptures can thus be interpreted both numerically and literally.

ANCIENT HISTORY

Numerology is one of the oldest analytical techniques in the world, and can be traced back to the Babylonians. The ancient Egyptians had their own numerology system, with occult powers attributed to each number; they used numerology as a means of understanding human psychology. Judaism holds what is probably the greatest key to the lore of numerology through the Kabbalah, a secret mystical text containing the philosophical science of numbers. In the 13th century, scholars of the Kabbalah developed the Gematria, a method of interpreting the Bible whereby inferences were drawn from the numerical value of the letters of the Hebrew alphabet. Using this method, Kabbalist scholars would search for hidden meanings in the text of the Old Testament.

THE CHRISTIAN TRADITION

Numbers have long had great symbolic spiritual significance in the Christian tradition. In the Middle Ages, numbers and geometry found their way into nearly every aspect of cathedral design, from the number of pillars in the choir to the layout of the façade. Number symbolism also features heavily in Christian theology. Some well-known examples include the two natures of Christ (human and divine), the Trinity, the four points of the Cross, the triple six (the number of the beast or the antichrist), the seven virtues and vices, the nine choirs of angels, and the twelve Apostles or disciples. The number thirteen, commonly thought of as the number of bad luck, symbolizes faithlessness and betrayal—the number of Apostles plus Judas.

The geometric design of the great cathedrals built during the Middle Ages and there-after reflect the awe and respect in which the power of numbers was held.

PYTHAGORAS

There is no doubt that the Greek philosopher and mathematician Pythagoras (*c.* 580-500 BC) is the father of Western numerology in the form that we know it today. Pythagoras believed that the world is built upon the power of numbers. In his words, "everything is numbers and to know numbers is to know thyself." According to Pythagorean theory, everything in the universe is composed of mathematical patterns, and thus all things can be expressed in numbers that correspond to universal vibrations. In this way, Pythagoras believed, numbers are the keys that can unlock the secrets of the universe and nature. It was Pythagoras who laid down the basic tenets of Western numerology, which operates by reducing compound numbers down to the nine primary numbers, each of which is assigned a particular meaning and symbolism. According to this methodology, all names and birth dates can be reduced to numbers in order to determine the personalities and destinies of individuals.

THE MIDDLE AGES

In medieval times, numerology was known as arithomancy or numeromancy, and was used for predicting the future. It was also used widely in conjunction with astrology and divination. One method of divination involved using Tablets of Fate (see pages 48-53), upon which numbers were cast in order to divine the possible answers to certain questions that an individual wanted answered. One of the most well-known numerologists during these times was Dr. John Dee. Dr. Dee was the official court magician of Queen Elizabeth I, and she relied heavily upon his divinatory powers. He was even asked to work out the most auspicious date for her coronation.

Although there are many numerological systems, the Pythagorean system for calculating personal numbers is the most popular today.

CHINESE NUMEROLOGY

The ancient Chinese developed one of the earliest binary number systems, derived from the *I Ching*, or the Book of Changes. This system uses two basic lines—a yin (broken line) and a yang (unbroken line)—to draw up sixty-four symbols. The lines are first translated into numbers and then into symbolic answers to spiritual questions. According to traditional Chinese numerology, odd numbers are "yang" and masculine, and relate to heat, fire, the sun, daytime, and the color white; they also forecast good fortune. Even numbers are "yin" and feminine, and are ascribed to cold, water, the moon, darkness, and to the color black; they relate to the earth, and symbolize openness.

INDIAN NUMEROLOGY

In India, numerology is used widely in *vaastu*, or sacred architecture. Before a house is built, its measurements are checked carefully, as the numbers derived from each calculation are symbolic representations of gods or goddesses who can bestow good or bad fortune upon the occupant.

Why numerology works

One of the basic tenets of Western numerology is that everything in the world is constantly vibrating with energy. Numbers are viewed as symbols of the constant cycle of energy, and are thought to reveal the patterns of life itself. Each number has its own unique vibrations, and each represents specific powers and opportunities. According to numerology, the numbers that are ascribed to each individual (particularly through their birth date and name) form a template for the energy in that person's life. Through awareness of the powers and principles of numerology, each individual can discover how to change the energy surrounding his or her life to achieve a harmonious vibration and reach his or her maximum potential.

NUMBERS AND MUSICAL NOTES

In the film Close Encounters of the Third Kind, *musical notes were the universal language and the means of communication between human beings and extra-terrestrials.*

Numbers are like musical notes; each has a vibration and an effect. When we speak numbers aloud, we release their powerful vibration into the cosmos. When we write numbers, they represent various symbolic meanings. Numbers are a universal language that will no doubt be spoken by the first aliens that visit us from another world. They may speak a different verbal language and have completely different social conventions, but their basic knowledge of numbers will be the same as ours, as science in every form uses numbers at its most basic level. The makers of the film *Close Encounters of the Third Kind* were correct to have had the alien spaceship conversing in musical notes, each note representing a number. The spaceship was, of course, speaking in mathematics, the universal language.

NUMBERS IN EVERYDAY LIFE

Virtually every aspect of our everyday lives depends on numbers, from our bank card to our car license plate, and from the currency with which we buy our groceries to our telephone number. Indeed, numbers are the framework within which we live our lives. Many objects which we consider essential to our quality of life also depend on numbers. For example, every page in a book has a number; there is a bar code on the back cover, without which the book could not be sold; there is a price on most books that is expressed in numbers; there is an International Standard Book Number for identification; and there is a copyright date expressed in numbers. Without numbers, it is fair to say that life as we know it would be considerably different—in all likelihood, much more difficult.

CONTROLLABLE AND UNCONTROLLABLE NUMBERS

From the moment we are born, each and every one of us is given a series of numbers in order to set ourselves apart from our fellow human beings. Most of these numbers are uncontrollable in the sense that they are allocated, probably at random, by an official or a computer. These numbers include those on our passport, bank account, Internal Revenue Service reference, birth certificate, marriage certificate, and, finally, our death certificate. These numbers are important—indeed, we cannot function without them—yet we cannot choose them ourselves. Nor, of course, do we have any choice as to our birth date. There are, however, some numbers over which we do have some control: those which correspond to the letters in our name. Although we are given a name at birth, we are perfectly free to change it, alter its spelling, or adopt a nickname. We can also change our names after marriage, as many women choose to do. By making such a change, we can alter our vibrational patterns and thus change many facets of our lives—everything from our personality to our destiny.

Chapter 1 Principles of Western Numerology

IN THE WESTERN SYSTEM OF NUMEROLOGY, WHICH IS BASED ON THE PYTHAGOREAN METHOD, EACH LETTER OF THE ALPHABET IS GIVEN A NUMBER BETWEEN 1 AND 9. BELOW IS A CHART THAT SHOWS THE ALLOCATION OF NUMBERS FOR EACH LETTER OF THE ROMAN ALPHABET.

Each of the nine numbers has its own special symbolism and meaning. As you progress through the book and learn how to figure out your personal numbers, you will need to refer back to the explanation of the nine numbers that follows.

The meaning of the nine numbers

Below is an at-a-glance guide to the meaning of the nine numbers:

1	strong, ambitious, innovative, active, creative
2	artistic, gentle, thoughtful, inventive, charming, intuitive
3	energetic, disciplined, talented, successful, independent, controlling
4	steady, practical, enduring, rebellious, unconventional, isolated
5	lively, pleasure-seeking, impulsive, quick-tempered, entrepreneurial
6	reliable, trustworthy, loving, caring, resolute, communicative
7	spiritual, introverted, psychic, lucky, restless, intuitive
8	successful, obstinate, individual, intense, difficult, rebellious
9	active, determined, quarrelsome, courageous, dangerous

1

NUMEROLOGY NAME: MONAD

The number 1 represents the Sun. It is the number of strength, individuality, and creativity. People with this number will never lack confidence or need reassuring. They are straightforward, bright, and honest people who love being out in the world and enjoy moving forward in life. They are natural leaders and innovators, seek challenge, and have a great need to be in the limelight. In its positive aspect, the number 1 is honest and upright; in its negative aspect, it is domineering and bossy. It is the sign of the saint and the tyrant, the saviour and the dictator. Number 1 people have endless energy and enthusiasm, and others who are less outgoing may find them intimidating and exhausting. Number 1 people can often, however, feel isolated and lonely. They strive to please others, but frequently fail owing to their belief that they are always right. Thus, their life lesson is to learn diplomacy and how to get along with others.

People with a Birth Number of 1 tend to possess great strength and endurance, and make solid leaders because of these qualities.

REPRESENTED DAY	SUNDAY
COLOR	RED
CAREERS	DESIGN, INVENTING, TEACHING, WRITING
KEY ATTRIBUTES	ACTIVE, RESOLUTE, TENACIOUS, CONFIDENT
NEGATIVE ASPECTS	INTOLERANT, CRITICAL, ARROGANT
SOCIAL ASPECTS	QUIET, INDEPENDENT

NUMEROLOGY NAME: **DUAD**

Number 2 people tend to be very emotional, and sometimes overly sensitive. Ecstatic one minute and upset the next, their mood swings are wild and unpredictable.

REPRESENTED DAY	MONDAY
COLOR	ORANGE
CAREERS	NURSING, ANY AREA OF HOSPITALITY, ART, THERAPY
KEY ATTRIBUTES	DIPLOMATIC, CREATIVE, INTUITIVE, EMOTIONAL
NEGATIVE ASPECTS	PASSIVE, DECEITFUL, DEPRESSIVE
SOCIAL ASPECTS	OUTGOING, FRIENDLY, SUPPORTIVE

Number 2 represents the Moon. It is the number of creativity, femininity, and gentleness. The typical number 2 person is more concerned with emotions than action. They are usually charming, sensitive, and intuitive. They are also changeable, and can adapt to virtually any situation. They get along very well with other people, and are caring and supportive. Number 2 people are typically diplomatic and like a peaceful life. This can lead to problems, however, as they prefer to avoid taking responsibility or making decisions. They are romantic and idealistic—sometimes overly so—and have a clear vision of what life should be like. Number 2 people have problems with self-confidence at times, however, and can be reluctant to see ideas through.

NUMEROLOGY NAME: **TERN**

Number 3 represents the family and the planet Jupiter. It is also the number of the Trinity. In ancient times, it was regarded as the perfect number, as it represents time, matter, and space; length, breadth, and depth; and solid, liquid, and gas. It was also linked to the triangle, which is the symbol of logic, intellect, and reason. Three is also the number of success and completion. Number 3 people know how to see projects through, always meet their deadlines, and are energetic and disciplined. They are independent and like to work hard, achieving success by overcoming odds and adversity. They enjoy a challenge, and will often seek out difficult situations so that they can be seen as trouble-shooters. They are also talkative and are very sure of themselves. Those with this number are freedom-loving and strong, organized and enthusiastic, and optimistic and tenacious. They can, at times, be slightly indifferent to the feelings of others, and tend to brush aside opinions somewhat briskly.

Punctuality is the mark of a true number 3 person, in both social and work contexts.

REPRESENTED DAY	TUESDAY
COLOR	YELLOW
CAREERS	ENTREPRENEURSHIP, LAW, BUSINESS, SALES, COMMUNICATIONS
KEY ATTRIBUTES	ENERGETIC, SUCCESSFUL, TALENTED, PUNCTUAL
NEGATIVE ASPECTS	PROUD, CONTROLLING, INTERFERING
SOCIAL ASPECTS	OUTGOING, TALKATIVE, GREGARIOUS

NUMEROLOGY NAME: QUATERNION

Number 4 represents the planet Uranus as well as the four seasons, the points of the compass, and the four elements. It is the number of reliability and steadfastness. Those with this number are practical and down-to-earth. In fact, earth is the best word to describe the number 4. Number 4 people are earthy in humor and life, robust and strong, and enduring and plucky. They enjoy the good things in life in abundance, and like to indulge themselves. Hedonist by nature, they enjoy experiences and sensations, and have little interest in accumulating material possessions. Although number 4 people can be bombastic and opinionated, they are always enthusiastic and full of life. They enjoy their own company, and don't suffer fools easily. The typical number 4 person may only have a few close friends rather than a lot of casual acquaintances and may be considered introverted. Number 4 people have great loyalty to both people and ideas. They are adept at processing abstract thoughts and turning them into logical, sensible opinions.

REPRESENTED DAY	WEDNESDAY
COLOR	GREEN
CAREERS	MATHEMATICS, ARCHITECTURE, ENGINEERING
KEY ATTRIBUTES	DEPENDABLE, TRUSTWORTHY, ENDURANCE, STAMINA
NEGATIVE ASPECTS	UNEMOTIONAL, IMPATIENT, RECKLESS
SOCIAL ASPECTS	UNDEMONSTRATIVE, RECLUSIVE, UNCONVENTIONAL

Most number 4 people prefer their own company to that of others, and like to tune the world out whenever possible.

NUMEROLOGY NAME: QUINCUNX

Number 5 represents the planet Mercury. It is the number of the senses and of social graces. People with this number are witty and charming, and are full of enthusiasm and life. Others find them good company and like being around them, as they are able to cheer everyone up by their presence alone. Change is a key word for number 5 people. They often experience a great deal of upheaval in their lives, all of which they adapt to easily and readily. They tend to recover quickly from adversity and bounce back easily from setbacks. Number 5 people are very good with words, and find it easy to learn languages. They like to exercise their intellectual capacity, and find puzzles and games challenging and enticing. Some number 5 people have quick tempers, however, and can be highly strung at times. They don't like being stuck in a rut, and will go downhill quickly if caught in one.

REPRESENTED DAY	THURSDAY
COLOR	BLUE
CAREERS	PUBLIC RELATIONS, ADVERTISING, ACTING, JOURNALISM, MANAGEMENT
KEY ATTRIBUTES	SENSUOUS, CHANGEABLE, IMPULSIVE
NEGATIVE ASPECTS	NERVOUS, HIGHLY STRUNG, EASILY BORED
SOCIAL ASPECTS	FUN LOVING, SOCIABLE, LOQUACIOUS

Many number 5 people love to exercise their minds, and become bored easily.

6

NUMEROLOGY NAME: **HEXAD**

Number 6 represents the planet Venus. It is the number of harmony, beauty, balance, and perfection. Those with this number are reliable and trustworthy, romantic and sensual, and attractive and cheerful. They are very home-based, and like organizing and being in charge of a family, but their secret love is performing for others—acting or singing is often in their bones. They are also softhearted and loving, and consider it their duty to care for underdogs and stray animals. Most number 6 people like working for charities and enjoy helping others less fortunate than themselves, especially those in need of physical assistance. They are very idealistic and rarely practical, especially about the causes of poverty or suffering. These people have an air of martyrdom about them, and expect everything to be alright without considering the practicalities of their charitable endeavors. They typically need to learn how to stand up for themselves more.

REPRESENTED DAY	FRIDAY
COLOR	INDIGO
CAREERS	FASHION, THEATER, CHARITY WORK, BEAUTY, MODELLING, MUSIC
KEY ATTRIBUTES	ROMANTIC, IDEALISTIC, SENSUAL
NEGATIVE ASPECTS	PASSIVE, DECEITFUL, DEPRESSIVE
SOCIAL ASPECTS	FRIENDLY, OUTGOING, SOCIABLE

Many number 6 people are hopeless romantics, and fall desperately in love quickly and easily. They also tend to be sensuous souls who appreciate beauty.

7

Number 7 represents the planet Neptune. It is the number of travel and the occult. Those with this number are intuitive and psychic, sensitive and spiritual, and pensive and philosophical. They may well exert considerable influence upon those around them by sheer force of personality without even realizing it. Number 7 people may seem a little cold and unemotional on the outside, but in reality nothing could be further from the truth—in fact, there is a great deal of turmoil and many intense feelings churning around inside of them. They are simply shy, and find it a bit hard to open up. Number 7 people invariably have others coming to them for advice and help, although they may well resent the intrusions into their time and space. Their opinions, no matter how reluctantly given, are always valued, and they are seen by others as mentally superior.

NUMEROLOGY NAME: SEPTENARY

REPRESENTED DAY	SATURDAY
COLOR	VIOLET
CAREERS	HEALING, COUNSELLING, THERAPY, CLAIRVOYANCE, ASTROLOGY, MUSIC
KEY ATTRIBUTES	INTUITIVE, INTELLECTUAL, PSYCHIC, UNIQUE
NEGATIVE ASPECTS	INTROVERTED, INSENSITIVE, UNSETTLED
SOCIAL ASPECTS	ALOOF, RESERVED

Mysticism and the occult are two of the typical number 7 person's favorite subjects. Others are in awe—and slightly afraid—of these people because of their psychic abilities.

8

NUMEROLOGY NAME: OCTAD

Number 8 represents the planet Saturn. It is the number of willpower and individuality, intensity and depth, and lessons and karmic duty. Those with this number may well be rebellious and unconventional, but these characteristics only drive them forward to accumulate great material success and wealth. They have an enormous amount of willpower, as well as individuality and strength of character. They know what needs to be done, and are usually very focused and goal-oriented. Number 8 people have great organizational abilities, and are naturally respected and looked up to. They are born leaders, and work well in a team—especially if they are in charge of it. They can push those under their command extremely hard, setting very high standards and producing spectacular results. Number 8 people are known for their courage, and they are not frightened to speak their minds—even if doing so makes them unpopular or controversial.

REPRESENTED DAY	SUNDAY
COLORS	DARK RED, CRIMSON, PURPLE, BLACK
CAREERS	THE MILITARY, BUSINESS, FINANCE, POLITICS, LAW, ENTREPRENEURSHIP
KEY ATTRIBUTES	ORIGINAL, INTENSE, IMAGINATIVE, DECISIVE
NEGATIVE ASPECTS	DOMINEERING, BLUNT, TACTLESS
SOCIAL ASPECTS	LEADING, ORGANIZING, SOCIABLE

Number 8 people are typically triumphant in virtually every task they undertake, owing to their incredible drive, confidence, and leadership abilities.

NUMEROLOGY NAME: NONES

Number 9 represents the planet Mars. It is the number of expression, both in the arts and in speech. Number 9 people have a great need to explore the depths of the human soul and express the universal poetry found there. They are creative, imaginative, sensitive, and intuitive people. They are also fighters and champions of the underdog. They like to take on causes—some of which may be unrealistic—and to aim for the goals that others would think unobtainable. People with this number have a great love of the exotic, strange, and freakish, and they may be attracted to people with odd quirks of personality and character. They can be very intense, and like to pick quarrels at times. These people are also active, and enjoy the thrill of danger and excitement. Number 9 people have problems at times with relationships, and tend to have trouble finding partners who will understand their need to express virtually everything they feel, see, and do.

REPRESENTED DAY	MONDAY
COLORS	WHITE, PINK
CAREERS	MUSIC, HYPNOTISM, EXPLORATION, TRAVEL, CLAIRVOYANCE, HEALING, WRITING
KEY ATTRIBUTES	QUIRKY, ACTIVE, COURAGEOUS, EMOTIONAL
NEGATIVE ASPECTS	DREAMY, UNREALISTIC, CLINGING, ADDICTIVE
SOCIAL ASPECTS	COMPANIONABLE, INTENSE, WACKY

Extreme sports and thrill-seeking activities are addictive for many people with number 9 personalities.

THE NUMBERS 1 THROUGH 9 ARE THE ESSENTIAL NUMBERS IN NUMEROLOGY. IN ORDER TO DO A PROPER NUMEROLOGICAL READING, ALL THREE PERSONAL NUMBERS MUST BE BROKEN DOWN TO A SINGLE DIGIT NUMBER. THERE ARE, HOWEVER, SOME NUMBERS THAT SHOULD BE READ FIRST AS A DOUBLE DIGIT, AND ONLY THEN REDUCED DOWN TO A SINGLE DIGIT. THESE ARE CALLED SECONDARY NUMBERS, AND THEY HAVE THEIR OWN SPECIAL MEANING AND SIGNIFICANCE: THEY ARE USED TO FLESH OUT THE READING FROM A SINGLE-DIGIT NUMBER. THE SECONDARY NUMBERS AND THEIR MEANINGS ARE SET OUT BELOW.

Secondary numbers

WORKING OUT YOUR SECONDARY NUMBER

If you work out your Birth Number, Known Name Number, or Full Name Number (see pages 26-31), and it comes out as a double-digit number, you may not want to reduce it down to a single-digit number so quickly. If the two-digit number is a number between 10 and 22, or the number 40, it is significant in its own right, and can add to the information obtained from your single-digit personal number. For instance, suppose your known name is Jon, which adds up to 12 (1 + 6 + 5). If you add the 1 and 2 together, reducing the number to a single digit, then Jon has a Known Name Number of 3, which means that he is energetic, disciplined, talented, successful, independent, and controlling. He is also, however, a 12 as a secondary number, which signifies completeness. Modify any of Jon's key characteristics above with the word "complete" and his reading becomes more detailed. We now know that Jon is talented, with the ability to complete projects. He is energetic, and his completeness gives him stamina. He is independent and successful, and feels a sense of wholeness in his life—in other words, his independence and success make him feel fulfilled.

THE SECONDARY NUMBERS

Below are the secondary numbers and their interpretations. The most powerful and strongly favored secondary numbers are 11, 12, 13, 22, and 40.

10	ATTAINMENT
11	SPECIAL MYSTICAL AWARENESS
12	COMPLETENESS
13	MAGIC AND MYSTERY
14	OVERCOMING OBSTACLES, STOICISM
15	OBSTINACY, RECKLESSNESS
16	EXCESSIVE CONFIDENCE
17	CREATIVITY, IMAGINATION
18	STRENGTH, ACHIEVEMENT
19	MISFORTUNE, SELF-DESTRUCTION
20	STEADYING INFLUENCE
21	FREEDOM, INDEPENDENCE
22	ACHIEVEMENT, SUCCESS
40	CHANGE, QUESTIONING

Secondary numbers can add a new perspective to single-digit personal numbers, and often help clarify their meanings and implications.

Your three essential numbers

1

YOUR BIRTH NUMBER

THE DATE, TIME, AND PLACE OF BIRTH ARE EQUALLY IMPORTANT FOR DIVINING PURPOSES IN NUMEROLOGY. FOR OUR PURPOSES, WE WILL CONCENTRATE ON THE BIRTH DATE NUMBER, ALSO KNOWN AS THE LIFE PATH NUMBER, WHICH REPRESENTS AND REFLECTS A PERSON'S INNER POTENTIAL. IF YOU FEEL LOST OR INDECISIVE, YOUR BIRTH NUMBER CAN HELP SET YOU ON THE RIGHT PATH. YOUR BIRTH NUMBER ALSO SHOWS YOUR INHERENT TALENTS AND CAPABILITIES.

Use the chart below to work out your Birth Number.

1	2	3	4	5	6	7	8	9
A	B	C	D	E	F	G	H	I
J	K	L	M	N	O	P	Q	R
S	T	U	V	W	X	Y	Z	

To figure out your Birth Number, add together the day, month, and year in which you were born, separating all the digits out.

→ For example, if your birthday were November 21, 1964, you would add it up the following way:

$$1+1+2+1+1+9+6+4 = 25$$

→ You would then reduce the number 25 down to a single-digit number:

$$2+5 = 7$$

→ Thus, your Birth Number would be 7. This number represents the character you were born with: your instincts, your karmic duty and lessons, your genetic makeup, your traits and flaws, and your life direction. If your Birth Number is 7, you are inherently spiritual, sensitive, and intuitive.

See pages 14-23 for an explanation of your Birth Number, and pages 24-25 for an analysis of your secondary Birth Number, if one exists for you.

If your Birth Number is 6, chances are that you are a born performer, and are happiest when all eyes are on you.

WHAT YOUR BIRTH NUMBER MEANS

Your Birth Number tells you what you have been brought into this world to explore and to find out—it is your Life Path revealed. It is where your soul resides, and is what motivates you. It is the underlying force in everything you do, even if you aren't conscious of it. Your Birth Number also tells you what your innate skills and talents are, thereby illuminating those aspects of yourself that you can depend upon to find success along the way.

HOW KNOWING YOUR BIRTH NUMBER CAN HELP YOU

By knowing your Birth Number—your genetic character, if you like—you will have a better understanding of where you are coming from, the underlying motivation that drives you, and your basic instinctive nature. This can be a great help when you need to make important life decisions, especially in the work realm. For instance, suppose 8 is your Birth Number. This number is all about power, control, willpower, and individuality. Say you are offered a job that requires you to take orders, and be obedient and submissive to your superiors. Knowing now what you do about your inherent nature, do you think you would be happy in this job? According to your Birth Number, the answer is a resounding no. Think of how much grief and stress you just saved yourself by doing this quick calculation.

OTHER PEOPLE'S BIRTH NUMBERS

Not only can you figure out your own Birth Number and thereby ascertain your own basic nature, you can also get a glimpse into anyone else's basic nature—so long as you know their birth date, that is. By working out your romantic partner's Birth Number, for instance, you can discover his or her basic motivation. This will allow you to have a better understanding of his or her emotions, which will no doubt lead to a stronger and more supportive relationship.

YOUR FULL NAME NUMBER

MOST PEOPLE CONSIDER A NAME TO BE NOTHING MORE THAN A LABEL, BUT THE REALITY IS VERY DIFFERENT. THE NAME YOU ARE BORN WITH IS YOUR PERSONAL TALISMAN. IT PROTECTS YOUR IDENTITY, AND CONNECTS YOU WITH THE VIBRATIONAL POWERS OF THE PREVIOUS GENERATION. YOUR FULL NAME NUMBER IS THE NUMBER DERIVED FROM THE NAME YOU WERE GIVEN AT BIRTH. IT CAN BE SAID TO REPRESENT THE FREUDIAN EGO AS THE EXPOSED AND CONSCIOUS OUTER SELF. THIS NUMBER TELLS YOU HOW YOU PRESENT YOURSELF TO THE OUTSIDE WORLD—AND WHAT OTHERS SEE.

CALCULATING YOUR FULL NAME NUMBER

Use the chart below to work out your Full Name Number.

1	2	3	4	5	6	7	8	9
A	B	C	D	E	F	G	H	I
J	K	L	M	N	O	P	Q	R
S	T	U	V	W	X	Y	Z	

Using the chart above, look up the numerical value of each letter of your full name. For instance, if your name were John Robert Smith, the letters would have numerical values as shown on the right.

→

J	O	H	N		R	O	B	E	R	T		S	M	I	T	H
1	6	8	5		9	6	2	5	9	2		1	4	9	2	8

→ Add the numbers together:
$1 + 6 + 8 + 5 + 9 + 6 + 2 + 5 + 9 + 2 + 1 + 4 + 9 + 2 + 8 = 77$

→ Add the two (or three) digits of the total together:
$7 + 7 = 14$

→ Reduce the number to a single-digit number:
$1 + 4 = 5$

Thus, your Full Name Number would be 5. Fourteen would be your secondary number, which could be used to flesh out your Full Name Number reading (see pages 24-25).

See pages 14-23 for an explanation of your Full Name Number, and pages 24-25 for an analysis of your secondary Full Name Number, if one exists for you.

Those with a Full Name Number of 1 are typically seen by others as ambitious and capable. At work, they are known as people who can be relied upon to get the job done.

Your Full Name Number can tell you what sort of person other people think you are. You may be surprised at their perceptions of you.

WHAT YOUR FULL NAME NUMBER MEANS

Your Full Name Number reveals your outer personality—how you present yourself to the outside world. It tells you how most people see you, and their likely impressions of you. This number is especially relevant to your career. It does not, however, tell you how the intimates in your life—those who know your real, inner personality—see you; this information is revealed by your Known Name Number (see pages 30-31).

HOW KNOWING YOUR FULL NAME NUMBER CAN HELP YOU

Knowing and understanding how others perceive you can help you in many facets of your life. In the workplace, for example, it can help prepare you for their reactions to your ideas, thereby making your presentation of these ideas more succinct. In a more general sense, knowing how others think of you can help you live up to their expectations—if you so desire. Or, if you discover that others attribute an unfavorable characteristic to you, you can always make an effort to change your ways—or your name (see page 42).

OTHER PEOPLE'S FULL NAME NUMBERS

It can also be helpful to know and understand the façade that others are presenting to the outside world. For example, if you are going for a job interview, it would certainly be helpful to be able to anticipate the interviewer's personality, which is bound to inform his or her interviewing style. Familiarity with, and an understanding of, the outer personalities of your friends, acquaintances, and co-workers can also improve your relationship with them.

YOUR KNOWN NAME NUMBER

Your known name is the name your lover, your family, and your close friends call you. It can be a nickname, a shortened form of your full name—even just an initial or your last name. The number that is derived from the letters of this name represents what Freud called the id: the hidden or unconscious self, or your inner personality.

CALCULATING YOUR KNOWN NAME NUMBER

First you must identify your known name. Your full name may be John Robert Smith, but everyone may not necessarily know you by that name. You may even be known by a few different names—perhaps your wife calls you John, for example, but your friends call you Bobby. By calculating the numerological values of each of these known names, you can find out which aspects of your personality are most valued. Let us look at an example.

Use the chart below to find your Known Name Numbers.

1	2	3	4	5	6	7	8	9
A	B	C	D	E	F	G	H	I
J	K	L	M	N	O	P	Q	R
S	T	U	V	W	X	Y	Z	

Add together the numbers of each your known names, as illustrated below.

J	O	H	N	
1	6	8	5	
B	**O**	**B**	**B**	**Y**
2	6	2	2	7

To calculate the Known Name Number for John, add the appropriate numbers together:

1 + 6 + 8 + 5 = 2 0
2 + 0 = 2

Thus, 2 is the number for the known name John; this number relates to artistic abilities and inventiveness.

To calculate the Known Name Number for Bobby, add the appropriate numbers together:

2 + 6 + 2 + 2 + 7 = 1 9
1 + 9 = 1 0
1 + 0 = 1

Thus, 1 is the number for the known name Bobby; this number relates to strength and activity.

This reading tells us that John's wife, who calls him John, values the artistic and inventive side of him, whereas his close friends, who call him Bobby, admire his strength and energy. The side of his personality that he reveals to his wife is perhaps softer and more emotional, whereas the side that he shows his friends is more outgoing and adventurous.

See pages 14-23 for an explanation of your Known Name Number, and pages 24-25 for an analysis of your secondary Known Name Number, if one exists for you.

Most people are known by more than one name; likewise, most people are valued and admired by different people for different characteristics.

WHAT YOUR KNOWN NAME NUMBER MEANS

Your Known Name Number is essentially your inner personality—the real you. You may show different sides of yourself to different people at different times, but your core personality is who you really are. Chances are, only those with whom you are intimate—your family, close friends, and lover—know you in this way. As might be expected, this number is particularly relevant in the realm of relationships.

HOW KNOWING YOUR KNOWN NAME NUMBER CAN HELP YOU

Sometimes, we are so busy being so many things to so many people that we forget who we really are, and what truly makes us happy in this life. By ignoring or forgetting about our true selves, we can become profoundly unhappy without ever realizing why. Knowing your Known Name Number and the characteristics associated with it can help you make sure that you never lose sight of the real you—the core of your true personality. In doing so, you can make sure that you remain faithful to yourself, as well as to your lover, friends, and family.

OTHER PEOPLE'S KNOWN NAME NUMBERS

Knowing other people's Known Name Numbers and their associated characteristics can be of use in many spheres of our lives, particularly in our relationships. Suppose, for example, that you are currently in a new relationship. It is still at the beginning stages, and so you and your partner are in the process of getting to know each other. Knowing your partner's Known Name Number can give you a fast track into his or her true personality, and can help you ascertain how he or she is really feeling. This type of information can help you become truly intimate more quickly, bringing the two of you closer together in a meaningful, honest way.

We present different sides of ourselves to different people, but it is those with whom we are most intimate that know us the best.

THE POWER OF VOWELS AND CONSONANTS

The vowels and consonants in both our full and known names have specific meanings that govern certain areas of our lives. For example, the first vowel in a person's full name can tell us what motivates him or her in his or her career, while the first vowel in a person's known name tells us what he or she is hiding in his or her relationships. The chart below gives us an at-a-glance reference for the numbers associated with each of the vowels, as well as a brief reading of their meanings in the contexts of relationships and careers.

VOWEL	NUMBER	RELATIONSHIP	CAREER
A	1	A need to control	Innovation and creativity
E	5	Indulgence and pleasure	Entrepreneurial skills
I	9	A love of danger, reckless behaviour	Communication and expression
O	6	A need for reassurance and a reluctance to trust	Trust and determination
U	3	A need for independence	Energy and talent

Take our old example of John Robert Smith, known to his friends as Bobby. Both his Full Name and Known Name Numbers have "O" as the first vowel. The letter "O" corresponds to the number 6, which is the number of romance, love, and devotion. From his full name (which relates to his career), we know that his underlying motivation at work derives from determination and trust. From his known name (which relates to his relationships), we can guess that Bobby is hiding a fear of falling in love. He is reluctant to commit himself to a romantic relationship, and needs his space and freedom. He is also in need of reassurance.

The vowels and consonants in our names can tell us a great deal about our real motivations, and can uncover our secrets.

LONG-TERM GOALS

If you add up the total of the vowels in your full name, you will arrive at your long-term goals. Suppose we use John Robert Smith again as an example. His vowel total is:

$$O + O + E + I$$
$$6 + 6 + 5 + 9 = 26$$
$$2 + 6 = 8$$

Thus, the number 8 is representative of John's long-term career path; 8 is the number of willpower, individuality, and intensity. This reading tells us that John's path will be difficult, but obtainable, so long as he maintains his vision and does not compromise. He will do well in any field of the law or the military—he could even combine the two and become a lawyer who specializes in military law.

RELATIONSHIP EXPECTATIONS

Consonants are the open side of our character and, as such, are much easier to interpret than vowels. By adding together the total of the consonants in our known name, we can find out what we expect from our relationships. By adding together the total of the consonants of our full name, we can discover what we expect in our working life.

For instance, the consonants in my known name are:

$$R + C + H$$
$$9 + 3 + 8 = 20$$
$$2 + 0 = 2$$

The number 2 derived from this reading tells me that I seek gentleness and charm in my relationships (see page 16 for more detail).

My full name consonants are:

$$R + C + H + R + D + C + R + Z$$
$$9 + 3 + 8 + 9 + 4 + 3 + 9 + 8 = 53$$
$$5 + 3 = 8$$

According to this number, I expect success and individuality in my working life (see page 22 for more detail).

According to one theory of numerology, our three personal numbers relate to the lessons we will learn throughout our lives. Many of these lessons will involve the development of our spiritual and moral selves.

Some numerologists believe that our Full Name Number tells us what we will accomplish in this lifetime.

HOW THE THREE NUMBERS LINK

Let us now summarize what we have learned from our personal numbers. We have found out that our Birth Number can tell us about our basic character and Life Path; our Full Name Number lets us know how we present ourselves to others and how they see us; and our Known Name Number illuminates for us our inner personality. Together, these three numbers can be expressed as a three-digit number, such as 4–5–7 or 9–3–1. There are 729 possible combinations of these three numbers. (A reading for each of these combinations is provided on pages 54-135.)

Because Pythagoras left only fragmented details of his system of numerology, there are many differences in numerological interpretation today. For the purposes of this book, we have chosen to interpret the meanings of our Birth, Full, and Known Name Numbers as stated above. We should be aware, however, that alternative numerological methods do exist.

COSMIC EXPRESSIONS

According to one school of numerology, our Birth Number tells us why we have been put on this earth. Specifically, it lets us know which karmic lessons we are supposed to be learning, and what our cosmic duties are. Our Full Name Number describes our purpose in life: where we are going, what we are supposed to achieve, and what our goals are in this life. It can also describe the method by which we choose to go down our Life Path. Our Known Name Number tells us about the nature of our relationships with others, as well as about our emotions, desires, and passions. It is also an indicator of how well we will enjoy the journey down our Life Path.

Suppose, for example, that your three-digit number is 4–5–1. Because 4 is your Birth Number, you can deduce that you have been put on this earth to learn endurance and stability. With 5 as your Full Name Number, you are likely to move down your Life Path in a lively, determined way. Because 1 is your Known Name Number, you might have trouble getting along with others along the way, so be prepared.

LESSONS

Some numerologists look at the three numbers as indicators of the lessons that we will learn in our lives. Our Birth Number represents our life lesson—the most important lesson that we have been put upon this earth to learn. Our Full Name Number tells us which lessons we will learn along the way. Finally, our Known Name Number imparts to us the lessons that we have yet to complete; these will become the lessons of our Birth Number in the next life.

Let's look at an example. Suppose your three-digit number is 8–3–9. The Birth Number 8 tells you that your karmic goal in this life is to learn how to work with others, to be less set in your ways, and to be more open to the opinions of others. Your Full Name Number of 3 tells you that as you travel along your Life Path, you need to learn how to be nicer and more gentle in your relationships with others. The number 9, your Known Name Number, tells you that you have yet to master the lessons of tolerance and forgiveness.

Chapter 2 Numerology for Daily Life

Once we understand the basic significance of numbers, we can begin to apply their meanings to everyday situations. Numerology can help us in many facets of our lives. It can tell us which colors are best suited to our home and wardrobe, and which days and years will be lucky for us. It can also tell us how we can change our names to bring luck and fortune into our lives, and what we should look for in the personal numbers of our business partners, friends, and lovers. We can even use numerology to see into the future.

COLOR AND NUMEROLOGY

Color is much more than a particular shade or hue. Like numbers, each color has its own vibration. Scientific studies have shown that some colors actually have an effect on our nervous system; for example, the color red stimulates us, while the color blue slows us down. It is no wonder that the advertising and entertainment industries employ colors to create certain moods and elicit desired reactions from viewers! Just as your personal numbers can give you insight into your true self, so certain colors can help you attract positive vibrations into your surroundings. By choosing a color that has a numerical vibration that is compatible with your personal numbers, you can intensify the ring of positive energy you have begun to build around yourself using these numbers.

FROM HEAD TO TOE

Just as you can choose some of your personal numbers, so you can choose the colors you wear in order to ensure that you send off the right vibrations in certain situations. For instance, if you are off enjoying a day on your own, you might wish to wear the color associated with your Birth Number—you will likely feel the most relaxed in the color that reflects your inherent characteristics. If you have a business meeting, however, you are probably best off wearing the color associated with your Full Name Number — so long as that is the image that you wish to project to the persons with whom you are meeting. For an outing with your family, close friends, or lover, you will probably be most comfortable wearing the colors that are linked to your Known Name Number.

Once you become more familiar with the system of numerology, you can play around with colors to suit your mood. Perhaps the idea of wearing orange to a business meeting is not suitable—well, you don't have to dress in orange from head to toe. A tie or scarf—or even orange socks—might be enough to tip the balance. If you think the appropriate color doesn't suit you, wearing a different shade of it will work just as well.

COLOR AT HOME

By decorating your home using colors that correspond to your personal numbers, you can attract positive vibrations into your most intimate surroundings. The colors in your bedroom should be those associated with your Birth Number, as you will likely find these colors restful on a basic, instinctive level. For those rooms in which you relax and unwind, such as a sitting room or a living room, it is best to use the colors affiliated with your Known Name Number. Those rooms in your home which guests are most likely to enter, such as a front foyer or a dining room, are best decorated using colors to reflect your Full Name Number. If the numerologically correct color for a particular room is not to your liking—a violet kitchen may be a bit much, for example—it will suffice to add details of the required color to the room. A decorative object here, a pillow there—even a single painted wall in the appropriate color will be enough to ensure the presence of the positive vibrations that you seek.

Above are the nine primary numbers and the particular colors that relate to them.

If your Birth Number is 6, then indigo is the color most suited to your innate characteristics. Recent studies have shown that the color indigo quiets the body and slows its functions down.

STYLE AND COLOR

Just as colors are linked to the nine primary numbers, so are clothing styles. By dressing in the style that corresponds to the appropriate personal number for a specific situation, you can amplify the positive vibrations surrounding you and increase your personal power. Dressing in the style that corresponds to your Full Name Number, for example, will ensure that you project the image that you wish to present to others, while wearing clothing of the style that is linked to your Birth Number or your Known Name Number will make you feel comfortable and confident.

1	sophisticated, understated, unique, daring, fashionable
2	smart, chic, matching, co-ordinated
3	relaxed, casual, light
4	practical, neat, orderly
5	sensual, unusual, sexy
6	modern, patterned, soft
7	sharp, crisp, natural
8	smart, businesslike, expensive
9	flamboyant, unconventional, youthful

The knowledge that Monday can be a day of conflict allows us to plan that day carefully.

A day for all types of activity, Tuesday is a good day to begin a task that you have been procrastinating.

LUCKY DATES

In numerology, each day of the week is associated with one or two of the primary numbers, and carries with it an energy that vibrates to that number. Similarly, each year of your life is linked to one of the primary numbers and its accompanying energy. By learning how to read this energy—that is, by figuring out your personal numbers—you can direct your affairs in such a way as to achieve the best possible results.

LUCKY DAYS

Below are the days of the week, their associated numbers, and a description of what one might expect each day to be like. Using this information, we can increase our good fortune by planning certain events on the most auspicious days for them. As well, because we know what to expect on each day, we can prepare ourselves for any potential difficulties that we might encounter. For example, suppose someone named Paul Smith wishes to plan a business meeting. His Full Name Number (the number linked to his career) is 2, so Monday is probably the best day for the meeting to take place. But because Monday can be a day for arguments and conflict, he should make a special effort to ensure that he and the other attendees work together calmly and co-operatively.

SUNDAY	1 & 8	a day of achievement and success
MONDAY	2 & 9	can be a day of conflict, but also calmness
TUESDAY	3	a day of general activity
WEDNESDAY	4	a day for hard work
THURSDAY	5	a day for physical activity
FRIDAY	6	a day for thought
SATURDAY	7	a day for learning

LUCKY YEARS

From your Birth Number, you can calculate which years will be particularly important for you. Suppose you were born on May 28, 1975. This gives you a Birth Number of 1. From the chart below, we can see that your 10th, 19th, 28th, 37th, and 46th years will be particularly joyous or noteworthy.

1	10th, 19th, 28th, 37th, 46th
2	11th, 20th, 29th, 38th , 47th
3	12th, 21st, 30th, 39th , 48th
4	13th, 22nd, 31st, 40th, 49th
5	14th, 23rd, 32nd, 41st, 50th
6	15th, 24th, 33rd, 42nd, 51st
7	16th, 25th, 34th, 43rd , 52nd
8	17th, 26th, 35th, 44th, 53rd
9	18th, 27th, 36th, 45th, 54th

Perhaps the hardest lessons should be saved for Saturday, a particularly good day for learning.

CHANGING YOUR NAME

According to Western numerology, a person's name is the code that encrypts his or her essential character. If you change your name, this will result in a change of the vibrations and energies that surround you. As this is the case, such a decision should not be taken lightly. If you do decide to take the plunge, however, the best advice is to choose a name that feels right to you intuitively, and then calculate the numerological meaning of this name to make sure that it has the qualities that you seek. Finally, be sure that you wish to discard the vibrations given off by your old name number—and that you can live up to those given off by the new one.

Many well known personalities have changed their names at some point in their lives, or have adopted nicknames that reflect their famous personae. Some examples are shown on page 136, to give you an idea of the power and implications of changing one's name.

CHANGING YOUR FULL NAME

As we have already seen, our career is associated with our Full Name Number (see pages 28-29). By changing our full name— the name we were given at birth—we can help ease ourselves into a new career, or change the way we present ourselves to our work colleagues. For example, suppose Jane Brown wishes to make a career change. We know from her Full Name Number of 3 that she is disciplined and successful in her present job. The problem is, she feels more like a 2: artistic and creative. She decides that she may want to change to a more creative job, and would like her Full Name Number to help her channel her creative energies towards this goal. So how can Jane Brown change her Full Name Number of 3 to a 2? One way to do so is to add an initial to her name: Jane Brown can become Jane H. Brown (with the addition of the "H," which is an 8, the 3 becomes an 11 (3 + 8), which is then reduced to a 2). Thus, Jane Brown has reconfigured her Known Name Number vibrations to ready herself for her new career. Other options for her would have been to add a complete middle name, or change her first or last name.

If you crave luxury and the high life, try changing your full name to alter the vibrations surrounding you that relate to your job. These new vibrations can set the scene for a more fulfilling and successful career.

Many women choose to change their last names when they get married, either taking their husband's last name or adding their husband's last name to their own last name. As we have seen, such a decision will impact the vibrations relating to how others see them, particularly in the work realm, and thus such a change should be considered carefully.

CHANGING YOUR KNOWN NAME

Perhaps you feel like you have outgrown a nickname, or that a name that others affectionately call you simply does not suit your personality. You will feel much better about yourself if you change your known name so that your corresponding Known Name Number reflects your true personality. Let's use Jane Brown again as an example. Suppose people have always called her Janey—a number 1, which is strong and active—but she has always felt more like a 7: spiritual and introverted. If we remove the "e" from the end of Jane, this would make her name Jan—a 7, which is a much more spiritual and intuitive number. Making this change is bound to make her feel better; she will finally feel that she is being true to her inner self.

Your Known Name Number also relates to your relationships (see pages 30-31). Suppose your Known Name Number is 7, which tells you that you are restless but thoughtful in your relationships, but the truth is that you are lively and pleasure-seeking in that regard—more like a 5. By changing your known name, and thus your Known Name Number, you can ensure that you are surrounded by the correct numerical vibrations.

It is important that your known name reflects your true inner self. If it doesn't, you will always feel like an imposter.

BUSINESS PARTNERS

By now it should come as no surprise that the relationships in your life—professional and otherwise—will be better if your numbers are compatible. If you are thinking about entering into a business partnership, you should always look at the Full Name Number of your prospective partner and make sure that you can work with someone with the associated character traits. Each of the nine primary numbers is linked to specific careers and professions. These are set out below.

1	design, inventing, teaching, writing, project management
2	nursing, any area of hospitality, art, therapy, accounting, collecting
3	entrepreneur, business, sales, communicating, anything to do with the arts
4	science, mathematics, architecture, engineering, anything to do with buildings, electricity, computers or technology
5	public relations, advertising, acting, journalism, management, anything to do with science, research or entertainment in a managerial position
6	fashion, theater, charity work, beautician, modelling, music, hairdressing, anything to do with caring for others
7	healing, therapy, counselling, clairvoyance, astrology, music, anything to do with being self-employed and running own business
8	the military, law, business, financial sector, politics, engineering, banking
9	music, hypnotism, exploration, travel, clairvoyance, healing, writing

If you are looking for a business partner in the arts, keep your eye out for someone with a Full Name Number of either 3 or 5.

FRIENDS, LOVERS, AND OTHER RELATIONSHIPS

Each of the nine primary numbers is affiliated with specific personal qualities. When looking for true love, a strong friendship, or any type of mutually beneficial relationship, it can help to ascertain whether your Known Name Number is compatible with that of your potential partner or friend. Of course, you and your potential partner or friend need not share the same Known Name Number in order to be compatible; indeed, different Known Name Numbers usually make for spicy, interesting relationships! A look at the person's characteristics will, however, let you know what you are getting into, and will help you decide whether or not you wish to proceed.

1	imaginative, strong, independent, active
2	kind, gentle, supportive, loving
3	controlling, energetic, independent, teacher
4	enduring, reliable, trustworthy, unconventional
5	pleasure-loving, indulgent, fun, easygoing
6	caring, articulate, steadfast, enduring
7	intuitive, romantic, sympathetic, thoughtful
8	intense, passionate, enthusiastic, impetuous
9	dynamic, sophisticated, flamboyant, liberal

LOVERS' COMPATIBILITY CHART

Certain numbers are particularly compatible with others in the romantic sphere. The chart below shows the best possible romantic matches.

1	2	3	4	5	6	7	8	9
4	5	6	7	8	9	1	2	3

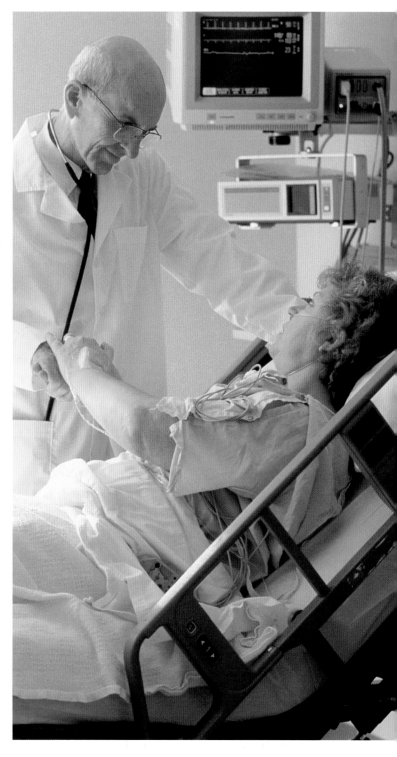

When choosing a health care specialist, it can be helpful to be able to anticipate his or her bedside manner. For example, a doctor with a Known Name Number of 6 will likely be more caring and sensitive than a doctor with a Known Name Number of 1.

NUMEROLOGY AND ASTROLOGY

The Sun

Astrology and numerology are similar systems in one very important respect: they are both used as tools to uncover the mysteries of life. Both systems are highly intricate, and both are based on mathematical truths that reveal the deeper universal order from which the fabric of life is woven. The primary belief that lies at the heart of astrology is that everything—from all living beings to the planets and stars—is essentially interconnected within a spiritual, energetic relationship.

The two main components in astrology are planets and signs. The planets symbolize the universal characteristics that all human beings possess. Mars, for example, symbolizes the warrior. The signs in astrology are named after their corresponding star constellations, and act as descriptions of how the planetary characters express their energies. For instance, the astrological sign of Aries, which is linked to the planet Mars, is typically associated with risk-taking and independence.

If you know your astrological sign, you can look up its associated number to gain a greater understanding of your nature. To the right is a list of the nine primary numbers, together with their corresponding signs and planets.

1	The Sun	Leo
2	The Moon	Cancer/Libra
3	Jupiter	Aquarius/Sagittarius
4	Uranus	Scorpio/Pisces/Aquarius
5	Mercury	Gemini
6	Venus	Libra
7	Neptune	Sagittarius/Cancer/Pisces
8	Saturn	Capricorn
9	Mars	Aries

The Moon

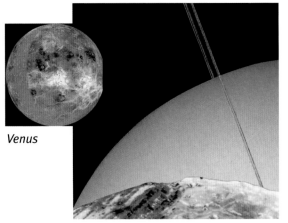

Venus

Uranus

THE DIVISION OF THE SIGNS

The twelve constellations, or astrological signs, are divisible into three groups: the cardinal, the mutable, and the fixed. The nine primary numbers are divided up into the same three groups. The cardinal signs are Aries, Cancer, Libra, and Capricorn; cardinal means doing and achieving. The three primary numbers associated with these qualities are 1, 4, and 7, which relate to the self and to new beginnings. The four

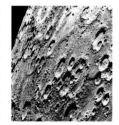

Mercury

fixed signs are Taurus, Leo, Scorpio, and Aquarius; fixed means resisting change. The three numbers associated with the fixed signs are 2, 5, and 8, which relate to how we appear to the outside world, as well as to morality. The four mutable signs are Gemini, Virgo, Sagittarius, and Pisces; mutable means changing and transforming. The three numbers associated with these signs are 3, 6, and 9, which have to do with service to others, relationships, and emotions.

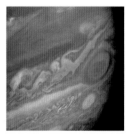

Jupiter

ASSESSING COMPATIBILITY

So how can we work with this new information? Well, once again it is useful for compatibility purposes. Suppose you are an Aries—this is a cardinal sign, and is associated with numbers 1, 4, and 7. You might well be advised to seek a life partner within the same number grouping. You will have a lot in common, share ideals, goals, and dreams, and will have an intuitive understanding of each other. That is not to say that partners within different groupings cannot work—they can. The difference is that they may have more hurdles to overcome.

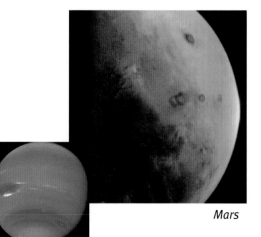

Mars

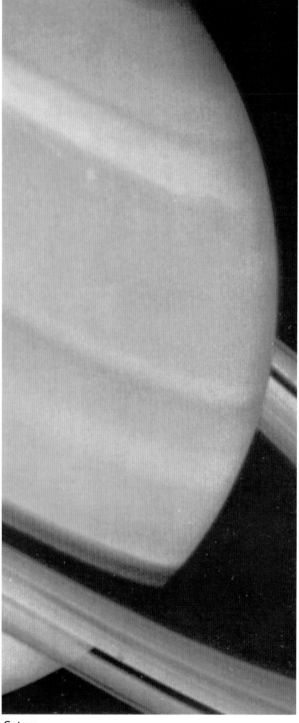

Saturn

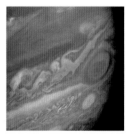

Neptune

Tablets of Fate

EACH TABLET HAS ITS OWN AREA OF CONCERN: THE EARTH TABLET IS USED FOR ASSESSING WHETHER YOU SHOULD ASK THE QUESTION AT ALL; THE MOON TABLET IS USED FOR QUESTIONS ABOUT THE ENVIRONMENT; THE TABLET OF VENUS IS TO BE CONSULTED REGARDING QUESTIONS RELATING TO ROMANCE; THE SUN TABLET IS USED FOR QUESTIONS ABOUT TIME AND THE FUTURE; THE TABLET OF MARS SHOULD BE ASKED CAREER-RELATED QUESTIONS; THE TABLET OF JUPITER IS MEANT FOR QUESTIONS RELATING TO LUCK AND FORTUNE; AND THE TABLET OF MERCURY CAN BE ASKED TRAVEL AND COMMUNICATIONS QUESTIONS.

USING THE TABLETS

In ancient times, the tablets would be printed on a thin sliver of bone or leather. If you are making your own tablets, however, a piece of card cut into the appropriate shape with the numbers written upon it will do (use the illustrated tablet shapes below and on the following pages as a reference). After you have cut the card into the appropriate shape, stick a toothpick or a pencil through the middle of it. Use each tablet as follows: ask your question, then spin the card around the toothpick or pencil, close your eyes, and stop the card from spinning by placing your finger firmly upon it. The

answer to your question is based on the number your finger has landed upon and how the number appears to you: upright or reversed. If the position of the number is unclear—if it lands on its side, for example—you should try again until you get a clear direction. Before you ask any questions, however, you must always refer first to the Tablet of Earth. This is the basic tablet that tells you whether it is a good time to ask your question—and whether you should be asking it at all.

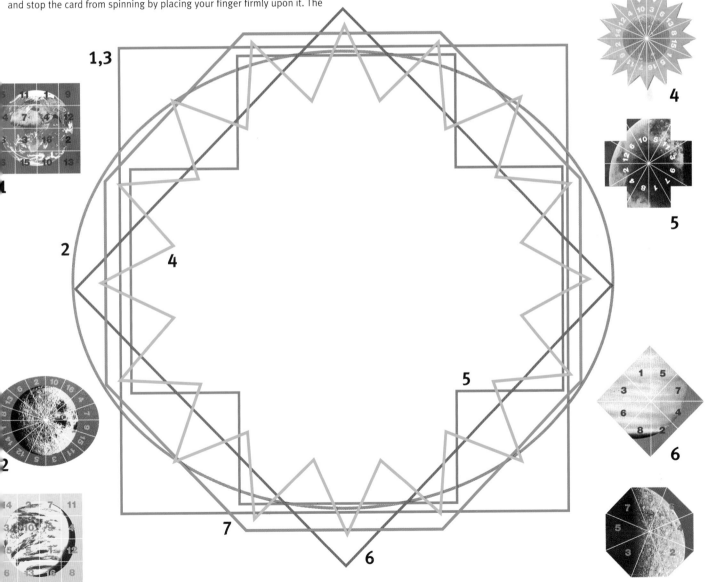

THE TABLET OF THE EARTH

This tablet should be consulted before you ask any question at all. If the tablet tells you to wait and ask your question later, or not to ask it at all, you are well advised to listen to it.

Number	Upright	Reversed
1	yes, now	wait 1 day
2	try tomorrow	wait 2 days
3	think very carefully before you ask	wait 3 days
4	you already know the answer	wait 4 days
5	simplify your question	wait 5 days
6	act quickly	wait 6 days
7	wait a little while before asking	wait 7 days
8	change your question	wait 8 days
9	you aren't in the right frame of mind to ask	wait 9 days
10	the answer will clarify things	wait 10 days
11	the answer will only cause you upset	wait 11 days
12	the answer will surprise you	wait 12 days
13	the answer will delight you	wait 13 days
14	ask only one question today	wait 2 weeks
15	question why you want to know	wait a month
16	if you do not ask you cannot know	do not ask ever

THE TABLET OF THE MOON

You may ask this tablet questions regarding your environment and immediate surroundings. For example, you can ask such questions as "Should I change my residence?" or "Can I redecorate without losing the warm atmosphere I have created?"

Number	Upright	Reversed
1	leave things as they are	listen to your inner voice
2	you need to change yourself first	change nothing
3	your advice is faulty	are you clear about your objectives?
4	you need your partner's help	go it alone
5	you already know the answer	ask again tomorrow
6	act quickly	wait 6 days and ask again
7	be more trusting	trust no one at this time
8	change your question	it is not possible at this time
9	rephrase your question and ask again	be more patient
10	look for an unlikely solution	be wary of easy solutions
11	pay attention to the details	you have missed something important
12	yes, if you are thoughtful	do not undertake any changes
13	yes, go ahead	be very cautious
14	go wild	be more practical
15	be active and reckless	be very careful and proceed slowly
16	if you do not ask you cannot know	tell no one

THE TABLET OF VENUS

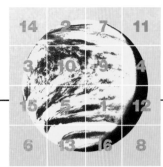

As might be expected, the Tablet of Venus should be asked questions pertaining to romantic relationships. This includes questions about a present romantic relationship, as well as those regarding a relationship you hope to have in the future.

Number	Upright	Reversed
1	lasting love	dying love
2	disagreements	agreements
3	you won't fool your beloved	you may well fool your beloved
4	try flattery	do not try flattery
5	be hasty	do not be reckless
6	blame yourself	blame your beloved
7	you are wrong to be jealous	you are right to be jealous
8	work hard to attain your heart's desire	there is nothing you can do at this time
9	be more serious about this	lighten up a little
10	your beloved is thinking of you	your beloved is not thinking of you
11	this will pass	this is permanent
12	your beloved misunderstood you	your beloved knows you too well
13	your beloved can be trusted	your beloved cannot be trusted
14	why are you doubtful?	you are right to be doubtful
15	speak your mind	keep silent at this time
16	you have found your soul mate	you are in danger of losing your soul mate

THE TABLET OF THE SUN

This tablet should be asked questions that have to do with time and timing. For example, if you wish to know the optimum timing with respect to a pertinent matter, this is the correct numerological oracle. This tablet can also be asked questions about the future.

Number	Upright	Reversed
1	in a while	in 1 year
2	never	most likely never
3	very unlikely	it is possible if you don't interfere
4	soon	not so soon
5	immediately	a very long time away
6	be patient	you are right to wait
7	next month	not for a few months
8	things will gradually change	things will suddenly change
9	it will improve quickly	it will worsen quickly
10	in two weeks	not for at least a month
11	sooner than you want	later than you want
12	next week	tomorrow, but are you ready?
13	in three days	in three months
14	don't ask at this time	what will you do when you know?
15	ask again tomorrow	do not ask again ever
16	yes, very soon	not for a long time

THE TABLET OF MARS

This tablet can answer questions about your career. Ask it questions relating to your present job, your career path, and whether it is wise for you to make a professional change.

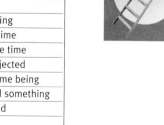

Number	Upright	Reversed
1	changes are imminent	there will be no change
2	be patient and you will be rewarded	you will not get any recognition
3	don't cheat	be very cautious
4	your star is ascending	your star is descending
5	be more trusting	trust no one at this time
6	you must put in more effort	you must put in more time
7	your ideas will be accepted	your ideas will be rejected
8	work as part of a team	work alone for the time being
9	you do not have all the facts	you have overlooked something
10	you are being groomed	you are being ignored
11	it is for the best	it is for the worst
12	you will attain great wealth	you are stagnating

The Tablet of Jupiter

Ask this tablet questions about luck and fortune. For example, you can ask it about what to expect from an upcoming event or project, or whether something you have been wishing for will happen.

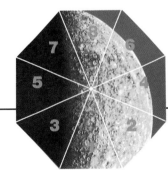

Number	Upright	Reversed
1	you are very lucky	you will experience misfortune
2	a surprise awaits you	you have to put something back
3	you will be rewarded	you can only work hard
4	you will be remembered	you will be forgotten
5	a new friend is waiting	an old friend is waiting
6	this is a good day for you	delay everything until tomorrow
7	be more open	be less trusting
8	it will all turn out right	you will be disappointed

The Tablet of Mercury

Consult this tablet for answers to your questions on the subjects of travel and communications. Queries regarding the timing and destination of a journey, as well as when you can expect to receive a certain communication, are appropriate for this tablet.

Number	Upright	Reversed
1	you will have a good journey	you will have a bad journey
2	good news awaits	bad news awaits
3	don't delay	put everything off
4	you already know the answer	be very wary
5	don't question, just go	you must be honest with yourself
6	tomorrow you will know	you are not ready yet
7	you received good advice	you received bad advice
8	you will be happy when you get there	don't go

CHAPTER 3 Unique 3-Digit Personality Guide

On the next 81 pages you will find over 700 3-digit combinations of character and personality assessments. To look up yours, turn to the page that has your Birth Number and your Full Name Number and then look at the relevant box for your Known Name Number reading. You can also find out the 3-digit numbers of the most compatible partners for you in both love and business by looking directly below your Known Name Number reading.

With a Birth Number of 1, you already know that you are extremely confident, as well as bright, honest, and sociable. With a Full Name Number of 1 as well, it is obvious to others that you possess these impressive characteristics. Your Known Name Number reading below is a deeper examination of your personality, and reveals the real you.

BIRTH NUMBER
1
1
FULL NAME NUMBER

Those in need can always depend upon you to come to their rescue, Known Name Number 6.

KNOWN NAME NUMBER

1 You are the epitome of strength and ambition. Your leadership qualities are renowned and you are busy and creative. Learn to chill out a bit more. You may be a little too forceful.
COMPATIBLE LOVE PARTNER - 444
COMPATIBLE BUSINESS PARTNER - 666

KNOWN NAME NUMBER

2 You are strong, busy, and artistic. You work hard and manage to get your ideas across with flair and gusto. You work well if left alone with your creative imagination.
COMPATIBLE LOVE PARTNER - 445
COMPATIBLE BUSINESS PARTNER - 667

KNOWN NAME NUMBER

3 You are active, creative, and extremely disciplined, which means you will work hard enough to get the job done—no matter what. You are independent and like to be in charge.
COMPATIBLE LOVE PARTNER - 446
COMPATIBLE BUSINESS PARTNER - 668

KNOWN NAME NUMBER

4 Your somewhat innovative but unconventional ideas are ahead of their time; you must wait for the rest of the world to catch up. One day, you will be proven right. You are very practical and logical.
COMPATIBLE LOVE PARTNER - 447
COMPATIBLE BUSINESS PARTNER - 669

KNOWN NAME NUMBER

5 If you spent as much time and effort on work and close personal relationships as you do on parties and pleasure-seeking, you would accomplish a lot more—and be much happier. You should settle down a bit.
COMPATIBLE LOVE PARTNER - 448
COMPATIBLE BUSINESS PARTNER - 661

KNOWN NAME NUMBER

6 As a public speaker you have no equal. You know how to put your ideas across extremely well and can be very persuasive. You have a great passion for helping people less fortunate than yourself.
COMPATIBLE LOVE PARTNER - 449
COMPATIBLE BUSINESS PARTNER - 662

KNOWN NAME NUMBER

7 If the world was looking for another religious prophet or teacher it would come straight to you. You are extremely knowledgeable about what makes people tick and could genuinely lead us all to salvation.
COMPATIBLE LOVE PARTNER - 441
COMPATIBLE BUSINESS PARTNER - 663

KNOWN NAME NUMBER

8 It's simply no good butting your head up against a brick wall. You are clever enough to know that, so why not stop? You have good ideas and people would listen to them more if you weren't so difficult.
COMPATIBLE LOVE PARTNER - 442
COMPATIBLE BUSINESS PARTNER - 664

KNOWN NAME NUMBER

9 Indiana Jones probably had the same 3-digit combination as you: active, adventurous, brave, reckless, dedicated, and extremely courageous. Go for it—the world exists to be conquered by you.
COMPATIBLE LOVE PARTNER - 443
COMPATIBLE BUSINESS PARTNER - 665

BIRTH NUMBER

1
2

FULL NAME NUMBER

A Birth Number of 1 indicates that you were born with confidence to spare. You are a natural leader and a talented innovator. With a Full Name Number of 2, you can be sure that you are seen by others as the creative type. They also see in you a charming and sensitive soul. Only you know if your outer self meshes with your inner self, however. Check your Known Name Number below to see if this is the case.

KNOWN NAME NUMBER

1 You are strong but gentle, energetic but not ruthless, forceful but compassionate. You are the gentle giant, always ready to help others and to be of service. Thank you.

COMPATIBLE LOVE PARTNER - 454
COMPATIBLE BUSINESS PARTNER - 676

KNOWN NAME NUMBER

2 You move through this world with such confidence and ease that the rest of us are a little jealous. Try to hide a few of your talents so we don't feel so inadequate.

COMPATIBLE LOVE PARTNER - 455
COMPATIBLE BUSINESS PARTNER - 677

KNOWN NAME NUMBER

3 Everything you do seems so easy because you never panic or get stressed. You are laid-back, chilled out, and extremely confident. All that you have ever wanted has been provided and you have not had to struggle.

COMPATIBLE LOVE PARTNER - 456
COMPATIBLE BUSINESS PARTNER - 678

KNOWN NAME NUMBER

4 You are an ideas rebel— always looking for the next invention, the next wacky concept, or the next brilliant innovation. You have an enormously imaginative and creative mind. Make sure it doesn't go to waste.

COMPATIBLE LOVE PARTNER - 457
COMPATIBLE BUSINESS PARTNER - 679

KNOWN NAME NUMBER

5 You look like a shady character that hangs around hotel lobbies—until asked to leave, whereupon you reveal that you are really a private investigator. Your disguise is awesome and fools all of us.

COMPATIBLE LOVE PARTNER - 458
COMPATIBLE BUSINESS PARTNER - 671

KNOWN NAME NUMBER

6 You cannot take on all of the world's ills and not suffer yourself. You care so much, so deeply, that you need to take a break and make some time for yourself. Learn to be more selective about your causes.

COMPATIBLE LOVE PARTNER - 459
COMPATIBLE BUSINESS PARTNER - 672

No one really knows what lurks behind the exterior you present to the world. You are a master of disguise and a true enigma, Known Name Number 5.

KNOWN NAME NUMBER

7 You are charming, ambitious, and thoughtful. You are also a restless soul, with an avid curiosity about other cultures. You will travel the world seeking the ultimate answer to the ultimate question. Good luck.

COMPATIBLE LOVE PARTNER - 451
COMPATIBLE BUSINESS PARTNER - 673

KNOWN NAME NUMBER

8 You are a very creative and artistic individual who speaks the truth no matter what the consequences. You may find a little diplomacy and tact helpful. It goes further than bluntness and honesty—at times, anyway.

COMPATIBLE LOVE PARTNER - 452
COMPATIBLE BUSINESS PARTNER - 674

KNOWN NAME NUMBER

9 Galileo was right, but he had to recant. Was he a coward or a hypocrite? You must also choose. You may well be right, but is the world ready for you? You are well aware that your ideas are shocking to some.

COMPATIBLE LOVE PARTNER - 453
COMPATIBLE BUSINESS PARTNER - 675

You love a good challenge, don't you, Birth Number 1? Your confident, bright nature may intimidate some people, however, so make sure that you are not being too bossy. Luckily, given your Full Name Number of 3, people see you as an independent person who works hard, and they admire your ability to overcome the odds. Do you really feel this confident and capable, or is it all an act? Check your Known Name Number below to learn more about yourself.

BIRTH NUMBER 1

FULL NAME NUMBER 3

KNOWN NAME NUMBER

1 It might be a good idea occasionally to take some time out to think before you act. You are very headstrong and reckless, and you need to look ahead to the future more often.

COMPATIBLE LOVE PARTNER - 464
COMPATIBLE BUSINESS PARTNER - 686

KNOWN NAME NUMBER

2 Children adore your ability to motivate and lead them. You have a unique gift and should use it more often. You are an inspirational teacher, and have a gentle charm and strong presence.

COMPATIBLE LOVE PARTNER - 465
COMPATIBLE BUSINESS PARTNER - 687

KNOWN NAME NUMBER

3 The chances of you actually reading this are remote, as you pretty well know everything already, don't you? But do you really? Isn't there a chance that you may have missed something?

COMPATIBLE LOVE PARTNER - 466
COMPATIBLE BUSINESS PARTNER - 688

KNOWN NAME NUMBER

4 You are strong, practical, and have tremendous powers of endurance and stamina. It might be an idea to stop and think about what you are doing from time to time, but you are a person of action above all else.

COMPATIBLE LOVE PARTNER - 467
COMPATIBLE BUSINESS PARTNER - 689

KNOWN NAME NUMBER

5 Watch that temper of yours and give people a chance to speak their minds to you in safety. You can be intimidating to others because you are so forthright and have such strong views. Go in peace.

COMPATIBLE LOVE PARTNER - 468
COMPATIBLE BUSINESS PARTNER - 681

KNOWN NAME NUMBER

6 People trust you, as you have a very gentle, knowing way about you. Make sure you don't destroy that trust by being too headstrong or too reckless. You care about others and can be very kind.

COMPATIBLE LOVE PARTNER - 469
COMPATIBLE BUSINESS PARTNER - 682

You are usually in the game for the long haul, Known Name Numbers 4 and 8, and do not like to quit until the race is won.

KNOWN NAME NUMBER

7 You have a talent for knowing exactly what people are thinking. To what use will you put this secret knowledge? Are you to be trusted with the inner thoughts and feelings of others? I certainly hope so.

COMPATIBLE LOVE PARTNER - 461
COMPATIBLE BUSINESS PARTNER - 683

KNOWN NAME NUMBER

8 You have carved a niche for yourself through your formidable strength and stamina. Now what are you going to do? Take some time out to think about the answer to this question—don't jump the gun.

COMPATIBLE LOVE PARTNER - 462
COMPATIBLE BUSINESS PARTNER - 684

KNOWN NAME NUMBER

9 We know you like your independence, so what's the beef? We know you are headstrong and outgoing, and have no wish to curb your freedom. Relax and stop being so darn argumentative.

COMPATIBLE LOVE PARTNER - 463
COMPATIBLE BUSINESS PARTNER - 685

BIRTH NUMBER
1
4
FULL NAME NUMBER

Those of you with a Birth Number of 1 inherently possess endless energy, stamina, and enthusiasm. Instead of finding you exhausting, however, we know from your Full Name Number of 4 that others see this zest for life as an indication of your robustness and strength. But this isn't the complete picture of your personality—your Known Name Number reading below provides the final piece to the puzzle.

Your strange ideas are interesting, Known Name Number 2, but they do not inspire confidence. Disguise your eccentricity if you wish to be taken seriously.

KNOWN NAME NUMBER 1

You cannot fail to succeed, as you have more ideas in a day than we have in a lifetime. You will surely roll some of them into a successful business and be very wealthy one day.

COMPATIBLE LOVE PARTNER - 474
COMPATIBLE BUSINESS PARTNER - 696

KNOWN NAME NUMBER 2

By being as eccentric as you are, you only draw attention to your unconventional ideas. Better to blend in more if you want to make headway. Learn to adopt a disguise.

COMPATIBLE LOVE PARTNER - 475
COMPATIBLE BUSINESS PARTNER - 697

KNOWN NAME NUMBER 3

You are very ambitious, but your success will depend upon whether you can learn to be a little more diplomatic and flexible. Can you change? If not, you may become isolated.

COMPATIBLE LOVE PARTNER - 476
COMPATIBLE BUSINESS PARTNER - 698

KNOWN NAME NUMBER 4

Don't worry—all that effort and hard work will not be in vain. Your reward is coming, your exertions will be praised, and your entitled success will follow. Just keep your head down and don't ask—yet.

COMPATIBLE LOVE PARTNER - 477
COMPATIBLE BUSINESS PARTNER - 699

KNOWN NAME NUMBER 5

Wait a little while and the world will be ready to accept your ideas. Don't push. Don't argue. Be patient. Carry on exactly as you are, as you are right and you know it. It's just a question of time.

COMPATIBLE LOVE PARTNER - 478
COMPATIBLE BUSINESS PARTNER - 691

KNOWN NAME NUMBER 6

Your three key words are strong, steady, and resolute. That's you. You work hard, play hard, and get on with the job at hand. You have a reputation for being a bit serious, but apart from that, you will get there.

COMPATIBLE LOVE PARTNER - 479
COMPATIBLE BUSINESS PARTNER - 692

KNOWN NAME NUMBER 7

You have quite a knack for being intuitive about all the wrong things. Better to direct your talents to a more appropriate cause and stop interfering where you may not be wanted. Save your talents for bigger things.

COMPATIBLE LOVE PARTNER - 471
COMPATIBLE BUSINESS PARTNER - 693

KNOWN NAME NUMBER 8

Ah, the rebel of the numerology world. What can we say to you that you will listen to? Nothing. Carry on the way you are going and you will alienate all your friends—if you haven't done so already.

COMPATIBLE LOVE PARTNER - 472
COMPATIBLE BUSINESS PARTNER - 694

KNOWN NAME NUMBER 9

White-water rapids hold no fear for you. You have more courage than is needed in this world, and are happiest when bungee jumping, climbing a mountain, or canoeing the Amazon. This world is too tame for you.

COMPATIBLE LOVE PARTNER - 473
COMPATIBLE BUSINESS PARTNER - 695

In its positive aspects, the Birth Number 1 is honest and upright. In its negative aspects, however, it is domineering and bossy, and can be quite intimidating. Those of you with Full Name Numbers of 5 have thankfully learned to keep these negative aspects in check; others see you as socially graceful. Indeed, you are a bit of an enigma. Your Known Name Number below can help you solve your own mystery.

BIRTH NUMBER 1
FULL NAME NUMBER 5

KNOWN NAME NUMBER

1 You are the party organizer par excellence. You have a flair for knowing what people need to relax and kick back. You can use this talent to run a successful business, or squander it all on indulgence—your choice.

COMPATIBLE LOVE PARTNER - 484
COMPATIBLE BUSINESS PARTNER - 616

KNOWN NAME NUMBER

2 You think you are always right, but haven't you over-looked something? Don't you often miss the vital clue because you are in such a rush to get things done? Learn to listen better and to look more closely.

COMPATIBLE LOVE PARTNER - 485
COMPATIBLE BUSINESS PARTNER - 617

KNOWN NAME NUMBER

3 You are the rat of the numerological world—inquisitive, busy, businesslike, quick, and a born opportunist. No opportunity passes you by without you making a profit from it. You care for your family extremely well.

COMPATIBLE LOVE PARTNER - 486
COMPATIBLE BUSINESS PARTNER - 618

KNOWN NAME NUMBER

4 Rebellious, impulsive, active, and strong: these are your key words. Take these words not only as praise, but also as a caution about being too reckless and rebellious. It's time you developed a little bit of tact and diplomacy.

COMPATIBLE LOVE PARTNER - 487
COMPATIBLE BUSINESS PARTNER - 619

KNOWN NAME NUMBER

5 For some of us, this is a learning experience. For you, however, it is purely fun. This is a life off for you and you can coast as much as you want without concern. Enjoy.

COMPATIBLE LOVE PARTNER - 488
COMPATIBLE BUSINESS PARTNER - 611

You can't rescue every stray dog—or person, Known Name Number 6.

KNOWN NAME NUMBER

6 Taking home stray dogs may seem like a good idea at the time, but your house will quickly fill up with hungry canines. Be more selective and only rescue those who will really appreciate it.

COMPATIBLE LOVE PARTNER - 489
COMPATIBLE BUSINESS PARTNER - 612

KNOWN NAME NUMBER

7 On the outside, you are busy and sociable; but inside, you are shy and retiring. Don't worry, I won't tell anyone your secret. You handle this obvious imbalance extremely well and are coping adequately.

COMPATIBLE LOVE PARTNER - 481
COMPATIBLE BUSINESS PARTNER - 613

KNOWN NAME NUMBER

8 Don't be quite so quick to be defensive when criticized. People are trying to help you, not hinder you. Heed what they have to say and you will improve yourself. Don't listen and you will alienate them.

COMPATIBLE LOVE PARTNER - 482
COMPATIBLE BUSINESS PARTNER - 614

KNOWN NAME NUMBER

9 You like being busy and active, but is it all just a distraction to stop you from thinking? You will have to face your inner demons one day—better to get it over with now. You have the courage, so what's stopping you?

COMPATIBLE LOVE PARTNER - 483
COMPATIBLE BUSINESS PARTNER - 615

BIRTH NUMBER **1**
6 **FULL NAME NUMBER**

With a Birth Number of 1, nothing pleases you more than going out into the world and exercising your formidable creativity. You are a true individual, as well as a leader and innovator. Perhaps others follow you so willingly because they find you trustworthy, as indicated by your Full Name Number of 6. Check your Known Name Number below to complete the picture of the complicated being that you are.

KNOWN NAME NUMBER

1 If you are not a politician, then what are you wasting your time on? You have a caring side that needs an outlet, and politics takes all of your communication skills into account. Run for office next time around.

COMPATIBLE LOVE PARTNER - 494
COMPATIBLE BUSINESS PARTNER - 626

KNOWN NAME NUMBER

2 Strong, reliable, and charming—that's you. You'd make a great daytime TV talk show host. You make people feel at ease, and they open up to you in an extraordinary way. Don't abuse this wonderful talent.

COMPATIBLE LOVE PARTNER - 495
COMPATIBLE BUSINESS PARTNER - 627

KNOWN NAME NUMBER

3 You can make a fortune simply by being clever at getting your ideas across. You have tremendous communication skills and a wealth of good ideas. Be confident and go for it.

COMPATIBLE LOVE PARTNER - 496
COMPATIBLE BUSINESS PARTNER - 628

Others appreciate the solidity of your friendship and your quiet dignity, Known Name Number 6.

KNOWN NAME NUMBER

4 Many new ideas are ridiculed before they become accepted. This is the nature of things and you cannot fight it. Be patient. Your time is coming. Hold fast to your bright vision and you will be rewarded.

COMPATIBLE LOVE PARTNER - 497
COMPATIBLE BUSINESS PARTNER - 629

KNOWN NAME NUMBER

5 If only you would see projects through, you'd be very successful. You have little stamina and you run out of enthusiasm too quickly. This will improve as you age, but practice some diligence in the meantime.

COMPATIBLE LOVE PARTNER - 498
COMPATIBLE BUSINESS PARTNER - 621

KNOWN NAME NUMBER

6 People rely heavily on your strength and steadfast-ness. You are their tower of fortitude—a virtual rock. But who finds time for you? Start thinking about yourself for once—you need a confidante and companion too.

COMPATIBLE LOVE PARTNER - 499
COMPATIBLE BUSINESS PARTNER - 622

KNOWN NAME NUMBER

7 You should be writing books like this one. You have the talent, the intuition, the stamina, the perseverance, and the skill. So what's holding you back? Ah, so you lack confidence. Get some and go for it.

COMPATIBLE LOVE PARTNER - 491
COMPATIBLE BUSINESS PARTNER - 623

KNOWN NAME NUMBER

8 You are ambitious, successful, resolute, and very creative. You are also a bit intense and have trouble getting along with people. We are not the machines that you love, so treat us a little more kindly please.

COMPATIBLE LOVE PARTNER - 492
COMPATIBLE BUSINESS PARTNER - 624

KNOWN NAME NUMBER

9 You are more than happy to descend into the very jaws of hell to rescue others. Take care lest your love of danger gets you into trouble. Be a little more cautious, but keep on being caring and loving.

COMPATIBLE LOVE PARTNER - 493
COMPATIBLE BUSINESS PARTNER - 625

You do not take orders well, Birth Number 1. You always want to be in charge, as you know you are usually the best person for the job. If 7 is your Full Name Number, these innate characteristics are confirmed; others constantly come to you for advice because they believe in you, and see you as mentally superior. Your Known Name Number below can tell you a bit more about your true colors.

BIRTH NUMBER 1

FULL NAME NUMBER 7

KNOWN NAME NUMBER

1 You are very determined and headstrong, and have a great sense of purpose. You have valuable work to do and need to get on with it, assuming you have spent some time exploring the world. There will come a time when you need to teach.

COMPATIBLE LOVE PARTNER - 414

COMPATIBLE BUSINESS PARTNER - 636

KNOWN NAME NUMBER

2 Channel your energies into travel and think carefully before you select a destination. Seek to learn about the world we live in and how you may be of help. You are capable of charming the whole world if you learn to smile more often.

COMPATIBLE LOVE PARTNER - 415

COMPATIBLE BUSINESS PARTNER - 637

KNOWN NAME NUMBER

3 You must not expect everyone to do your bidding all the time. Allow others to express themselves more, and you will be surprised at how much they are drawn to you.

COMPATIBLE LOVE PARTNER - 416

COMPATIBLE BUSINESS PARTNER - 638

KNOWN NAME NUMBER

4 If you must rebel, at least find something worthwhile to fight against. You are intuitive and strong, and need to concern yourself with the big issues of the day rather than the details.

COMPATIBLE LOVE PARTNER - 417

COMPATIBLE BUSINESS PARTNER - 639

KNOWN NAME NUMBER

5 If you concern yourself only with pleasure, make sure it is for the benefit of others as well as yourself. You are impulsive and headstrong, and seek to always have your own way.

COMPATIBLE LOVE PARTNER - 418

COMPATIBLE BUSINESS PARTNER - 631

KNOWN NAME NUMBER

6 Your inner strengths are directed toward caring for others. You have a natural, intuitive way of communicating advice and help, which comes from a very real and secure base. You are at ease when dealing with others less fortunate than yourself.

COMPATIBLE LOVE PARTNER - 419

COMPATIBLE BUSINESS PARTNER - 632

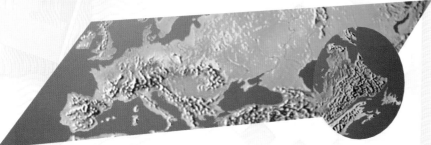

Travel is an important part of your karmic education, Known Name Numbers 1 and 2. Visiting other countries and learning about other cultures will help you grow as a person.

KNOWN NAME NUMBER

7 With 7 as both an inner and outer number, you are both blessed and cursed with an almost telepathic knowledge of what others are thinking. If you do not use this power wisely, it will bite you.

COMPATIBLE LOVE PARTNER - 411

COMPATIBLE BUSINESS PARTNER - 633

KNOWN NAME NUMBER

8 If you learn to curb your stubborn streak and listen to the advice of others, you will find great success in this life—but can you do this? You are a very intense individual who may be perceived as difficult and rebellious.

COMPATIBLE LOVE PARTNER - 412

COMPATIBLE BUSINESS PARTNER - 634

KNOWN NAME NUMBER

9 If anyone needed a hero, it might well be you they would turn to. You are intuitive, courageous, determined, and fearless—but you also pick fights unnecessarily and can be very quarrelsome.

COMPATIBLE LOVE PARTNER - 413

COMPATIBLE BUSINESS PARTNER - 635

BIRTH NUMBER

1

8

FULL NAME NUMBER

With a Birth Number of 1, you are above average in intelligence, which only adds to your innate confidence. You need to be careful, though, not to intimidate others, and should focus on being more diplomatic. This will be difficult, however, as you enjoy speaking your mind—indeed, others expect this sort of behavior from you, given that your Full Name Number is 8. Your Known Name Number below offers a glimpse into your inner personality.

KNOWN NAME NUMBER

1 You are very ambitious and aggressive. This is fine, just so long as you treat people kindly as your career progresses. If you don't, you will never truly enjoy the fruits of your labor.

COMPATIBLE LOVE PARTNER - 424
COMPATIBLE BUSINESS PARTNER - 646

KNOWN NAME NUMBER

2 Paranoia isn't a normal state to be in. They aren't out to get you, so relax. Be at one with your universe. It's okay to be you and to allow others to see your vulnerable side. Be trusting.

COMPATIBLE LOVE PARTNER - 425
COMPATIBLE BUSINESS PARTNER - 647

KNOWN NAME NUMBER

3 What a perfectionist you are. You like to control every aspect of life around you, and you seem to be able to get away with this terrible behavior. This is probably because of your creative genius. Lucky you.

COMPATIBLE LOVE PARTNER - 426
COMPATIBLE BUSINESS PARTNER - 648

KNOWN NAME NUMBER

4 No matter what anyone else says, you always go your own sweet way. Fair enough, just so long as you aren't sulking. Be free. Be independent. Be your own person. But do it all for the right reasons.

COMPATIBLE LOVE PARTNER - 427
COMPATIBLE BUSINESS PARTNER - 649

KNOWN NAME NUMBER

5 They see you as a dark star: mysterious and brooding, secretive and enigmatic. Is this the real you, or have you learned to hide your true self? Most of this darkness is an act—and one you are good at—but try being softer.

COMPATIBLE LOVE PARTNER - 428
COMPATIBLE BUSINESS PARTNER - 641

Don't step on others in your race up the ladder to the top, Known Name Number 1, or your nasty behavior will come back to haunt you.

KNOWN NAME NUMBER

6 You might be doing it your way and getting somewhere. But how about trying a little tact? You might get there quicker and with less stress. You communicate well and have a silver tongue.

COMPATIBLE LOVE PARTNER - 429
COMPATIBLE BUSINESS PARTNER - 642

KNOWN NAME NUMBER

7 You hammer away at life, and just when things seem at their worst a miracle happens and saves you—a door opens and you fall through. You are one very lucky individual. Why you should be so rewarded is a mystery.

COMPATIBLE LOVE PARTNER - 421
COMPATIBLE BUSINESS PARTNER - 643

KNOWN NAME NUMBER

8 Just because you are creative and artistic doesn't mean you can behave rudely or unkindly. You may be an intellectual giant, but you should learn to be a loving one as well.

COMPATIBLE LOVE PARTNER - 422
COMPATIBLE BUSINESS PARTNER - 644

KNOWN NAME NUMBER

9 You are like some old-fashioned movie tycoon with a big cigar and a tyrant's ego. You can be very ruthless. Lighten up a bit and give others a chance to speak. You might like what they have to say.

COMPATIBLE LOVE PARTNER - 423
COMPATIBLE BUSINESS PARTNER - 645

The Birth Number 1 makes for complex and contradictory individuals: it is the sign of the saint and the tyrant, the savior and the dictator. If your Full Name Number is 9, you are most likely on the saint and savior side of the fence. You have a great need to express yourself; others may even see you as a great poet. But your inner personality, as shown below in your Known Name Number reading, represents the real you.

BIRTH NUMBER **1**
FULL NAME NUMBER **9**

KNOWN NAME NUMBER

1 Your determination knows no bounds. You are going to succeed no matter what. The trouble is, what will you do when you get there? There will be nothing left to fight for. Slow down a bit and enjoy the ride.

COMPATIBLE LOVE PARTNER - 434
COMPATIBLE BUSINESS PARTNER - 656

KNOWN NAME NUMBER

2 Carry your vision with you and be kind to the little people along the way. You will be amply rewarded once you arrive at the place called success if you have behaved decently. But you already know this, don't you?

COMPATIBLE LOVE PARTNER - 435
COMPATIBLE BUSINESS PARTNER - 657

KNOWN NAME NUMBER

3 Whoa! You are a tornado, a tiger, a whirling dervish. You are a blur in people's sights —they can't get a handle on you. Slow down a bit and let's have a look at you.

COMPATIBLE LOVE PARTNER - 436
COMPATIBLE BUSINESS PARTNER - 658

KNOWN NAME NUMBER

4 You are the wild artist in the attic, the starving poet in the tower. But why? You have enough talent to earn a good living. So why this act? Come on down and be real with us.

COMPATIBLE LOVE PARTNER - 437
COMPATIBLE BUSINESS PARTNER - 659

KNOWN NAME NUMBER

5 You can't do everything yourself. At some point, you will have to accept some help, be it from a partner or a colleague. You will be happier if you stop trying to be everything to everyone.

COMPATIBLE LOVE PARTNER - 438
COMPATIBLE BUSINESS PARTNER - 651

KNOWN NAME NUMBER

6 You are the action person of the numerology world: resolute, steel-jawed, handsome, reckless, courageous, daring, and utterly fearless. That's all fine and well in the jungle, but in everyday life you are in danger of becoming a dinosaur.

COMPATIBLE LOVE PARTNER - 439
COMPATIBLE BUSINESS PARTNER - 652

You are as frenzied as a tornado, Known Name Number 3. Do yourself a favor and slow down, or you may become destructive—both to others and to yourself.

KNOWN NAME NUMBER

7 There is no point in playing any sort of spiritual games. Sure, you are intuitive and psychic, but it is in the use of such knowledge that true power resides. Be aware that power can be taken away if it is used unwisely.

COMPATIBLE LOVE PARTNER - 431
COMPATIBLE BUSINESS PARTNER - 653

KNOWN NAME NUMBER

8 You are like a wild alley cat—always ready to spit, bite, scratch, or cuss. Relax. We only want to be friendly and to get to know you a bit better. Give us a break and allow yourself to be stroked occasionally.

COMPATIBLE LOVE PARTNER - 432
COMPATIBLE BUSINESS PARTNER - 654

KNOWN NAME NUMBER

9 I would like to offer you some advice, but I'm afraid that you would bite my head off. If you would allow me to, I would suggest that you might win more influence if you learned to be a bit more diplomatic and tactful.

COMPATIBLE LOVE PARTNER - 433
COMPATIBLE BUSINESS PARTNER - 655

BIRTH NUMBER
2
FULL NAME NUMBER
1

If 2 is your Birth Number, you are innately a very gentle person, with a strong feminine side. You can also be highly emotional—sometimes to the point of inaction. Your Full Name Number of 1 indicates that others sometimes see you as a bit of a loner; you really must try harder to get along with people, both in your social life and at work. Your Known Name Number reading below will help you understand yourself a bit better.

KNOWN NAME NUMBER

1 Everything you do is based on your intuitive grasp of human nature. This can make you very clever or very cynical, depending on what you intuit. You have great drive, strength, and ambition.

COMPATIBLE LOVE PARTNER - 544
COMPATIBLE BUSINESS PARTNER - 766

KNOWN NAME NUMBER

2 If you aren't careful, you are in danger of losing touch with reality. Keep your feet planted firmly on the ground and try not to be so dreamy. You have great vision, but need to work hard in order to realize it.

COMPATIBLE LOVE PARTNER - 545
COMPATIBLE BUSINESS PARTNER -767

KNOWN NAME NUMBER

3 You are wonderful at translating your ideas into positive action; people respect your ability and give you their time because of this. Make sure you remain realistic.

COMPATIBLE LOVE PARTNER - 546
COMPATIBLE BUSINESS PARTNER - 768

KNOWN NAME NUMBER

4 You may need to tailor your ideas a little to become slightly more conventional. Doing so will get you farther, and shouldn't be seen as betraying your ideals. Don't be so rebellious.

COMPATIBLE LOVE PARTNER - 547
COMPATIBLE BUSINESS PARTNER - 769

KNOWN NAME NUMBER

5 If you don't settle down to some real work, you will squander all those dreams and visions. I know you feel compelled to daydream and procrastinate, but you really must get on with it.

COMPATIBLE LOVE PARTNER - 548
COMPATIBLE BUSINESS PARTNER - 761

KNOWN NAME NUMBER

6 Take some time out to think about what it is you want. You give so much time to others that there really isn't any left for you. Be more assertive about the demands that are put on you. Try saying no sometimes.

COMPATIBLE LOVE PARTNER - 549
COMPATIBLE BUSINESS PARTNER - 762

Make a greater effort to become part of the team, Birth Number 2.

KNOWN NAME NUMBER

7 It's no good always relying on luck to get you out of trouble. You need to be much more realistic and practical about everything and not so spiritual. Start being more proactive about the things that need to get done.

COMPATIBLE LOVE PARTNER - 541
COMPATIBLE BUSINESS PARTNER - 763

KNOWN NAME NUMBER

8 If you learn to work better with your colleagues and stop being quite so intense, you will find work more enjoyable, and you may even become part of a team. This is what you want, so why do you drive people away?

COMPATIBLE LOVE PARTNER - 542
COMPATIBLE BUSINESS PARTNER - 764

KNOWN NAME NUMBER

9 You are very determined and can swamp people with your need for reassurance and nurturing. Give others a little more space and they will respond to you better. You are very lively and need to calm down a little.

COMPATIBLE LOVE PARTNER - 543
COMPATIBLE BUSINESS PARTNER - 765

With both your Birth Number and your Full Name Number as 2, you really are as you seem: charming, sensitive, and gentle. You get along well with others, and are a great friend. People are always leaning on you for support. But only you know how you really feel about your designated role as nurturer. Perhaps you should spend more time taking care of yourself. Your Known Name Number reading below may shed some light on that subject.

BIRTH NUMBER
2
2
FULL NAME NUMBER

It's time you stopped freeloading off your friends and family and started earning a living, Known Name Number 5.

KNOWN NAME NUMBER

1 You have an amazing ability to think laterally. Use this talent to increase your creativity and you will go far. You are anxious for recognition rather than money, and this may be holding you back.

COMPATIBLE LOVE PARTNER - 554
COMPATIBLE BUSINESS PARTNER - 776

KNOWN NAME NUMBER

2 People may well take advantage of you if you don't learn to stand up for yourself a bit more. Your quiet, thoughtful nature is misinterpreted as weakness. Be tougher.

COMPATIBLE LOVE PARTNER - 555
COMPATIBLE BUSINESS PARTNER - 777

KNOWN NAME NUMBER

3 Your charm will get you as far as you want to go, and your artistic talent will provide a good living. But stop trying to be in charge all the time—allow others to speak up more.

COMPATIBLE LOVE PARTNER - 556
COMPATIBLE BUSINESS PARTNER - 778

KNOWN NAME NUMBER

4 Keep plugging away at your dreams and you will get there. Don't lose heart. The time just isn't quite right for your unconventional vision. It would be criminal to give up now, though, because you're nearly there.

COMPATIBLE LOVE PARTNER - 557
COMPATIBLE BUSINESS PARTNER - 779

KNOWN NAME NUMBER

5 Unless you stand to inherit a lot of money, you need to start earning a living or you will become a scrounger. Is this what you want? Of course not. Go out and get a job. You are growing old disgracefully.

COMPATIBLE LOVE PARTNER - 558
COMPATIBLE BUSINESS PARTNER - 771

KNOWN NAME NUMBER

6 People rely on you and trust your judgment. If you learn to use this talent properly, you will have a long and successful career. You need to learn how to speak up about what you know.

COMPATIBLE LOVE PARTNER - 559
COMPATIBLE BUSINESS PARTNER - 772

KNOWN NAME NUMBER

7 Whatever it is that you are trying to express can only be communicated once you have put it into words internally. You need to speak your words of wisdom to yourself before trying them out on others.

COMPATIBLE LOVE PARTNER - 551
COMPATIBLE BUSINESS PARTNER - 773

KNOWN NAME NUMBER

8 You are a unique individual and possess great charm. You can also be stubborn and difficult, but people forgive you and like you a great deal. You have a need to express yourself in an artistic way.

COMPATIBLE LOVE PARTNER - 552
COMPATIBLE BUSINESS PARTNER - 774

KNOWN NAME NUMBER

9 There is something you've always wanted to do, and now is the time to do it. Don't procrastinate. Take your courage in both hands and aim for the stars. What are you waiting for? Get on with it.

COMPATIBLE LOVE PARTNER - 553
COMPATIBLE BUSINESS PARTNER - 775

BIRTH NUMBER 2

FULL NAME NUMBER 3

The Birth Number 2 makes you innately a peacekeeper. You feel alarmed when people are fighting in front of you, and would do anything if they would only kiss and make up. This need to promote harmony is recognized by others; your Full Name Number 3 tells you that you are known as a troubleshooter, and are sought out as a mediator by quarrelling factions. Your Known Name Number below can help you discover if this is the real you.

KNOWN NAME NUMBER 1

There is nothing that holds you back. You are artistic, strong, ambitious, and energetic, and there is no doubt that you will go far. You have an aptitude for hard work, and this will always stand you in good stead.

COMPATIBLE LOVE PARTNER - 564
COMPATIBLE BUSINESS PARTNER - 786

KNOWN NAME NUMBER 2

You are inventive, talented, and thoughtful. If you apply yourself, you will achieve a great deal. You occasionally need to toughen up a bit, but the world could certainly use more people like you.

COMPATIBLE LOVE PARTNER - 565
COMPATIBLE BUSINESS PARTNER - 788

KNOWN NAME NUMBER 3

You wonder why people aren't more drawn to you, and yet you do nothing to encourage them. Your need for independence makes you seem remote and unobtainable. Try to be a little more approachable.

COMPATIBLE LOVE PARTNER - 566
COMPATIBLE BUSINESS PARTNER - 788

KNOWN NAME NUMBER 4

You can achieve your vision by the steady application of hard work, but if you remain so unconventional you will encounter problems. You may feel isolated— perhaps you need to make more of an effort to reach out to others.

COMPATIBLE LOVE PARTNER - 567
COMPATIBLE BUSINESS PARTNER - 789

KNOWN NAME NUMBER 5

You are one of those lucky people who can make money, attract lovers, and influence people—almost without trying. You have a natural gift for charm and sophistication, and are extremely quick-thinking.

COMPATIBLE LOVE PARTNER - 568
COMPATIBLE BUSINESS PARTNER - 781

KNOWN NAME NUMBER 6

Is there nothing that you won't do for others? You are so kind, so loving, and so helpful that you may feel slightly put upon at times. Try to be a little bit more selective about who you give your time to.

COMPATIBLE LOVE PARTNER - 569
COMPATIBLE BUSINESS PARTNER - 782

KNOWN NAME NUMBER 7

You love travel and will wander forever if you don't put down some roots. You are drawn to foreign places, and have a need to sense and experience the spiritual climate of other cultures. You are very restless.

COMPATIBLE LOVE PARTNER - 561
COMPATIBLE BUSINESS PARTNER - 783

KNOWN NAME NUMBER 8

You are artistic, energetic, and very successful. You have a marvelous ability to combine the creative with the practical and, although you can be rebellious, you are an efficient and hard worker.

COMPATIBLE LOVE PARTNER - 562
COMPATIBLE BUSINESS PARTNER - 784

KNOWN NAME NUMBER 9

You are managing your quarrelsome nature extremely well, and haven't lost your temper for ages. Well done. You are very caring and thoughtful, and are making a real effort to help other people. You make this world a better place.

COMPATIBLE LOVE PARTNER - 563
COMPATIBLE BUSINESS PARTNER - 785

If you would only reach out to others, Known Name Number 4, you wouldn't feel so alone.

You are by nature a diplomatic, peaceful person, but another side of you has a tendency to avoid making decisions. Indeed, your Birth Number 2 is marked by indecision. Thankfully, this is not how others perceive you. If your Full Name Number is 4, then you are seen as possessing a great loyalty towards ideas, which counteracts any hint of indecisiveness. Your true inner personality is revealed below in your Known Name Number reading.

BIRTH NUMBER
2
4
FULL NAME NUMBER

KNOWN NAME NUMBER
1 Without a life partner, you will flounder. You need to be part of a team of two, so get out there and find your soul mate. I know you have duties and responsibilities, but you must also think of your happiness.

COMPATIBLE LOVE PARTNER - 574
COMPATIBLE BUSINESS PARTNER - 796

KNOWN NAME NUMBER
2 Don't be frightened to speak your mind. I know you don't like to hurt people's feelings, but you really do need to make some changes. Be a little less charming and a little more ruthless.

COMPATIBLE LOVE PARTNER - 575
COMPATIBLE BUSINESS PARTNER - 797

KNOWN NAME NUMBER
3 As you know, you work hard and long hours, and are frequently exhausted. Take a break. Learn to relax a bit more and have some fun. You are in danger of being labelled a workaholic if you carry on at this rate. Take some time for yourself.

COMPATIBLE LOVE PARTNER - 576
COMPATIBLE BUSINESS PARTNER - 798

Until you find yourself a life partner, Known Name Number 1, you will never feel truly whole.

KNOWN NAME NUMBER
4 You have a lot of interesting ideas and are good at putting them into practical and realistic outlets. You are creative and inventive, but you need to curb your wilder excesses if you wish to be successful.

COMPATIBLE LOVE PARTNER - 577
COMPATIBLE BUSINESS PARTNER - 799

KNOWN NAME NUMBER
5 You need people around you—and you need to be part of a team—so stop pushing them away. You need them in order to flourish. Try to be a little less concerned with pleasure and pay more attention to your work.

COMPATIBLE LOVE PARTNER - 578
COMPATIBLE BUSINESS PARTNER - 791

KNOWN NAME NUMBER
6 You should be a counselor, but not a conventional one. You have a natural gift for helping people. You need to find an outlet for this talent, but avoid the traditional and go for the wacky or the new.

COMPATIBLE LOVE PARTNER - 579
COMPATIBLE BUSINESS PARTNER - 792

KNOWN NAME NUMBER
7 You have the wonderful ability to surf the cosmos and bring back spiritual ideas that inspire and motivate other people. Find a proper outlet for this incredible talent, and you are bound for success.

COMPATIBLE LOVE PARTNER - 571
COMPATIBLE BUSINESS PARTNER - 793

KNOWN NAME NUMBER
8 You are driven and goal-oriented. You work like a machine, and expect the same from others. Perhaps you need to realize that people are softer, more emotional, and need to be nurtured in order to get the best from them.

COMPATIBLE LOVE PARTNER - 572
COMPATIBLE BUSINESS PARTNER - 794

KNOWN NAME NUMBER
9 I know you are only trying to help, but you must try to find a more diplomatic way to get your ideas across. You think everyone should share your opinions, but you must make allowances for the views of others.

COMPATIBLE LOVE PARTNER - 573
COMPATIBLE BUSINESS PARTNER - 795

BIRTH NUMBER 2
FULL NAME NUMBER 5

What an optimist you are, you of the Birth Number 2! People have accused you of being too idealistic, but you know that it is possible to make the world a better place—if only people would try harder. We know from your Full Name Number of 5 that people see you as charming and graceful, which, of course, helps you attain your charitable goals. But are you really as angelic as you seem? Your Known Name Number below reveals your true personality.

KNOWN NAME NUMBER 1

You have a marvelous ability to integrate all the elements of mind, body, and spirit. You set a good example for the rest of us as to how to be both businesslike and creative, out in the world and well grounded.

COMPATIBLE LOVE PARTNER - 584
COMPATIBLE BUSINESS PARTNER - 716

KNOWN NAME NUMBER 2

If you go off on a tangent all the time and don't stick to the job, you will miss out on the success that is rightfully yours. Apply yourself to the task at hand and don't be so dreamy. Buckle down and get on with it.

COMPATIBLE LOVE PARTNER - 585
COMPATIBLE BUSINESS PARTNER - 717

KNOWN NAME NUMBER 3

You suffer from a curious apathy or loss of energy at times, and need to watch your diet carefully. You also should get more exercise and develop your strength. You need to say thank you to someone who loves you.

COMPATIBLE LOVE PARTNER - 586
COMPATIBLE BUSINESS PARTNER - 718

You always look on the bright side, Birth Number 2, no matter how bad things get. Perhaps this is because you are so at peace with yourself and the world around you.

KNOWN NAME NUMBER 4

You are not alone. Help is very near—you just haven't looked in the right place yet. Be more adventurous—you know that this makes sense for you. You have a rebellious side that needs to see more light.

COMPATIBLE LOVE PARTNER - 587
COMPATIBLE BUSINESS PARTNER - 719

KNOWN NAME NUMBER 5

A few less parties and a few earlier nights and you might achieve a lot more. You are very impulsive and are easily led astray. Look at your friends carefully and get rid of the ones that have a bad influence on you.

COMPATIBLE LOVE PARTNER - 588
COMPATIBLE BUSINESS PARTNER - 711

KNOWN NAME NUMBER 6

You are well known for your ability to get ideas across. You are a natural orator and are in demand due to your communication skills. You can be a bit unreliable, though, and may lose respect because of this.

COMPATIBLE LOVE PARTNER - 589
COMPATIBLE BUSINESS PARTNER - 712

KNOWN NAME NUMBER 7

You are like the fabled hare—quick-moving, shy, determined, and a bit restless. The hare also has a reputation for being ethereal and not quite of this world. You come across as the same.

COMPATIBLE LOVE PARTNER - 581
COMPATIBLE BUSINESS PARTNER - 713

KNOWN NAME NUMBER 8

There is a side of you that you are quite right to keep hidden: that darker, more mercurially aggressive part. You know you have a sharp tongue and can be very cutting. Work on keeping it under control.

COMPATIBLE LOVE PARTNER - 582
COMPATIBLE BUSINESS PARTNER - 714

KNOWN NAME NUMBER 9

You are determined to earn a reputation as a scoundrel. But is that what you really want? Perhaps it's time to curb this desire to be thought of as a troublemaker and to start expressing your artistic side.

COMPATIBLE LOVE PARTNER - 583
COMPATIBLE BUSINESS PARTNER - 715

With a Birth Number of 2, not only are you caring and gentle, you are also extremely intuitive, and possess great insight into the feelings of others. These qualities make you a great parent, sibling, or child. Add these qualities to the fact that your Full Name Number is 6, the number of domestication, and you are quite happy just staying home and caring for your family. Check below to see if your inner personality meshes with this reading.

KNOWN NAME NUMBER

1 If you could gather up the whole world in the palm of your hand and love us, you would be happy. Well, it's time you realize you can't. We won't let you. You would be better off finding a single cause to support.

COMPATIBLE LOVE PARTNER - 594
COMPATIBLE BUSINESS PARTNER - 726

KNOWN NAME NUMBER

2 You move through this world in a hazy vision of love and peace, like some Sixties hippie. Well, life ain't like that. You need to be more real and to get grounded. There is a lot of work to be done.

COMPATIBLE LOVE PARTNER - 595
COMPATIBLE BUSINESS PARTNER - 727

KNOWN NAME NUMBER

3 Inventive, loving, and talented—that's you. You care about people, and can often see ways to help them which they may have overlooked. Keep up the good work and you will no doubt be successful.

COMPATIBLE LOVE PARTNER - 596
COMPATIBLE BUSINESS PARTNER - 728

KNOWN NAME NUMBER

4 You may wonder why people don't take your advice more often when you are so ready and willing to give it. Perhaps they look at the proof of the eating rather than the pudding you offer.

COMPATIBLE LOVE PARTNER - 597
COMPATIBLE BUSINESS PARTNER - 729

KNOWN NAME NUMBER

5 You have a quick mind, but you need to apply yourself a little more to your goals. Stop expending your energies on so much self-indulgence and pleasure and start paying more attention to the serious stuff.

COMPATIBLE LOVE PARTNER - 598
COMPATIBLE BUSINESS PARTNER - 721

KNOWN NAME NUMBER

6 People trust you and bring their problems to you, and you are very good at giving them advice, helping them, and encouraging them to stand on their own two feet. Do the same for yourself occasionally.

COMPATIBLE LOVE PARTNER - 599
COMPATIBLE BUSINESS PARTNER - 722

Stop dedicating yourself to every cause you hear about and start concentrating on a select few, Known Name Number 9, and you will be more successful.

KNOWN NAME NUMBER

7 You don't move through this world like the rest of us. We deal with concrete facts, but you deal with feelings, intuitions, premonitions, hunches, and lucky omens. And who is to say that you are wrong to do so?

COMPATIBLE LOVE PARTNER - 591
COMPATIBLE BUSINESS PARTNER - 723

KNOWN NAME NUMBER

8 You can be very obstinate, especially with partners, which is a shame since you also have a very loving side. You just have this terrible need to win all arguments. You need to work on this competitive side of your nature.

COMPATIBLE LOVE PARTNER - 592
COMPATIBLE BUSINESS PARTNER - 724

KNOWN NAME NUMBER

9 You are determined to save the world, the whales, the kangaroos—even if none of them need saving. You devote a lot of energy to lost causes, and might want to start being a little more realistic in your endeavors.

COMPATIBLE LOVE PARTNER - 593
COMPATIBLE BUSINESS PARTNER - 725

BIRTH NUMBER

2

7

FULL NAME NUMBER

Some have accused you, Birth Number 2, of avoiding your responsibilities. Deep down, you know this is true, but you keep putting off making important decisions anyway—you just don't want to deal with the pressure. Your Full Name Number of 7 tells us that some might see you as cold and uncaring, even though you're not—you just want someone else to solve the problem. Your Known Name Number reading below shows how you feel about it all.

KNOWN NAME NUMBER

1 You are inventive, spiritual, and ambitious. I do hope you are not going to try to sell me a new religion or cult. You should be aware of the long-term results of your actions.

COMPATIBLE LOVE PARTNER - 514

COMPATIBLE BUSINESS PARTNER - 736

Stop behaving like a small child, Known Name Number 4—it's time to move on. You will be successful at whatever task you put your mind to.

KNOWN NAME NUMBER

2 You need to watch less TV and get out more. Join a club or two. Go on a vacation. Switch your computer off occasionally. Get some fresh air and exercise. I think you know what I'm saying.

COMPATIBLE LOVE PARTNER - 515

COMPATIBLE BUSINESS PARTNER - 737

KNOWN NAME NUMBER

3 You are active, imaginative, and very lucky. With your charm and talent, you can reach heights the rest of us only dream of. So what's holding you back? Perhaps you fear change too much. Be bold and take the plunge.

COMPATIBLE LOVE PARTNER - 516

COMPATIBLE BUSINESS PARTNER - 738

KNOWN NAME NUMBER

4 Inside you there is a small child crying out that life isn't fair. Just accept that it was never meant to be. The sooner you do, the quicker you can get on with your life. Be strong and real. You can be successful.

COMPATIBLE LOVE PARTNER - 517

COMPATIBLE BUSINESS PARTNER - 739

KNOWN NAME NUMBER

5 No one can ever quite get a handle on you. You are a very elusive being, a creature of the shadows and moonlight. You are a nebulous entity full of mystery and illusion—and you like it that way.

COMPATIBLE LOVE PARTNER - 518

COMPATIBLE BUSINESS PARTNER - 731

KNOWN NAME NUMBER

6 You have a genuine rapport with people that need caring and love. The trouble is, you may be one of those people yourself. So who cares for you? Don't be so accepting—stand up and demand the love that you deserve.

COMPATIBLE LOVE PARTNER - 519

COMPATIBLE BUSINESS PARTNER - 732

KNOWN NAME NUMBER

7 If you were any less grounded, you'd simply float away. Only your partner keeps you on earth, and you should be grateful for that. I guess you're not though, as you yearn to be free.

COMPATIBLE LOVE PARTNER - 511

COMPATIBLE BUSINESS PARTNER - 733

KNOWN NAME NUMBER

8 You are one of those rare people who can be in this world but not of it. You are able to put your talents for caring and sharing to use in a very successful and businesslike way. Well done.

COMPATIBLE LOVE PARTNER - 512

COMPATIBLE BUSINESS PARTNER - 734

KNOWN NAME NUMBER

9 There is something slightly dangerous about you. I'm not sure I would tell you my problems for fear you might use the information against me. This may, of course, just be your image. If so, you put on a good show.

COMPATIBLE LOVE PARTNER - 513

COMPATIBLE BUSINESS PARTNER - 735

You of the Birth Number 2 are very in touch with your feminine side. You have a wonderfully nurturing personality, lending your friends and lovers virtually endless support and an ever-ready shoulder to cry on. In fact, you are so good with others that you are, as your Full Name Number 8 tells us, a great leader. Everyone knows that sticking with you is a safe bet. Only your Known Name Number can tell you what's going on deep down inside.

BIRTH NUMBER
2
8
FULL NAME NUMBER

KNOWN NAME NUMBER

1 You are a tornado of energy and activity. But is it all show and no substance? Are you all wind and no weather? Show us that you can really achieve all that you claim and we will be convinced.

COMPATIBLE LOVE PARTNER - 524
COMPATIBLE BUSINESS PARTNER - 746

KNOWN NAME NUMBER

2 Whatever you turn your hand to comes out right. You could scribble a phone number on a piece of paper and sell it as a masterpiece. I envy your outrageous talent. You can also be a bit of a schemer.

COMPATIBLE LOVE PARTNER - 525
COMPATIBLE BUSINESS PARTNER - 747

KNOWN NAME NUMBER

3 So far, you have achieved a great deal by being difficult and intense. Perhaps now is the time to ease up a bit and relax. You may make some enemies if you don't learn to be a bit more pleasant.

COMPATIBLE LOVE PARTNER - 526
COMPATIBLE BUSINESS PARTNER - 748

KNOWN NAME NUMBER

4 You are rebellious when there is simply no need to be. You have the strength of character to throw off your old image of being a troublemaker and start doing some decent, hard work.

COMPATIBLE LOVE PARTNER - 527
COMPATIBLE BUSINESS PARTNER - 749

KNOWN NAME NUMBER

5 You are acquiring quite a reputation for being unreliable because you love to take so much time off. This isn't just at your work, but also in your relationships. Figure out why you need to escape so often.

COMPATIBLE LOVE PARTNER - 528
COMPATIBLE BUSINESS PARTNER - 741

KNOWN NAME NUMBER

6 Your artistic side is being displayed in a very individualistic way. Whether this is working for you only you can judge. If it is, keep on being wacky. If it isn't, you might try being a bit more conventional.

COMPATIBLE LOVE PARTNER - 529
COMPATIBLE BUSINESS PARTNER - 742

Stop being so subversive, Known Name Number 4. It's time you grew up and settled down.

KNOWN NAME NUMBER

7 Some like to wander because they are restless. Others feel a need to escape. But some, like you, wander for the sheer enjoyment of it. You are one of the genuine travelers who is out there for pleasure alone.

COMPATIBLE LOVE PARTNER - 521
COMPATIBLE BUSINESS PARTNER - 743

KNOWN NAME NUMBER

8 Successful, obstinate, and very charming. What a curious mix you are. On the one hand, there is this difficult side; but on the other, you do seem to be getting your own way—and very successfully, I might add.

COMPATIBLE LOVE PARTNER - 522
COMPATIBLE BUSINESS PARTNER - 744

KNOWN NAME NUMBER

9 Difficult and dangerous. That's you. But perhaps only I know that. Everyone else thinks you are a pussycat. But that's only because you are getting your own way right now. What happens when that stops?

COMPATIBLE LOVE PARTNER - 523
COMPATIBLE BUSINESS PARTNER - 745

BIRTH NUMBER 2

FULL NAME NUMBER 9

A gentle soul you are, Birth Number 2, but you lack self-confidence. Sometimes you feel incapable of seeing a project through, so you don't. This failure shakes your confidence even further, and the vicious cycle continues. You really shouldn't be so hard on yourself. Though your goals may be lofty, others admire you for having the courage to strive for them. Look to your inner personality, as expressed by your Known Name Number below, for strength.

KNOWN NAME NUMBER 1

You are thoughtful, ambitious, and very determined. You think you can get your own way pretty much all of the time—but you can't. You might need to be a little more diplomatic to achieve all you want to.

COMPATIBLE LOVE PARTNER - 534
COMPATIBLE BUSINESS PARTNER - 756

KNOWN NAME NUMBER 2

You are so charming it is dangerous. Is there no one who is immune to your enchantments and allure? It might be better if there were someone who could say no, as getting everything you want isn't good for you.

COMPATIBLE LOVE PARTNER - 535
COMPATIBLE BUSINESS PARTNER - 757

KNOWN NAME NUMBER 3

You see the road ahead as straight and direct, and it might well be. But allow for detours—this will make you more interesting and less possessed. You don't allow much to stand in your way, do you?

COMPATIBLE LOVE PARTNER - 536
COMPATIBLE BUSINESS PARTNER - 758

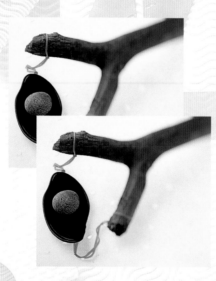

The Davids of this world can fight the Goliaths without your help, Known Name Number 6. Stop worrying about them and start looking out for yourself.

KNOWN NAME NUMBER 4

You aren't always right, you know. Oh, I'm sure you have considered the possibility and rejected it on the grounds that it couldn't be so. Perhaps if you listened a bit more, you might learn something.

COMPATIBLE LOVE PARTNER - 537
COMPATIBLE BUSINESS PARTNER - 759

KNOWN NAME NUMBER 5

If you spent as much time and effort patching up your romantic relationships as you do on your friendships, you might gain a little more love and respect. It's no good complaining if you don't lay the groundwork first.

COMPATIBLE LOVE PARTNER - 538
COMPATIBLE BUSINESS PARTNER - 751

KNOWN NAME NUMBER 6

What a bold little soul you are. Always ready to take on the Goliaths of this world to protect the Davids. But do they really need so much protection? Could they not fire the slingshot themselves?

COMPATIBLE LOVE PARTNER - 539
COMPATIBLE BUSINESS PARTNER - 752

KNOWN NAME NUMBER 7

Just because you have found the perfect way doesn't mean we all have to go the same route. Oh, I know it might be the right way, but please allow us to make our own mistakes. Stop preaching.

COMPATIBLE LOVE PARTNER - 531
COMPATIBLE BUSINESS PARTNER - 753

KNOWN NAME NUMBER 8

Go on, dig in your heels a bit more. But perhaps you are standing in quicksand, and digging in your heels is a really bad idea. Pointless telling you this though, isn't it? You are the most stubborn person imaginable.

COMPATIBLE LOVE PARTNER - 532
COMPATIBLE BUSINESS PARTNER - 754

KNOWN NAME NUMBER 9

Just because you have a good idea doesn't mean we all have to buy into it. It may not be practical or saleable. It may not be suitable. It may be ahead of its time. Stop arguing and think of something else.

COMPATIBLE LOVE PARTNER - 533
COMPATIBLE BUSINESS PARTNER - 755

The Birth Number 3 is characterized by success and completion in all spheres of life. You are a hard worker, and are driven to get the task at hand done—and done properly. You are seen by others as bright and honest, if a bit domineering and bossy, but you know that that's what it takes to get the job done sometimes. Your Known Name Number below can tell you what's really going on inside your head while you're busy acting professional.

BIRTH NUMBER
3
FULL NAME NUMBER
1

KNOWN NAME NUMBER

1 You have a lot of drive and ambition; all you have to do now is to find a direction to channel all that energy into. Could be this won't happen until later in life, when you have a family to think about and care for.

COMPATIBLE LOVE PARTNER - 644
COMPATIBLE BUSINESS PARTNER - 866

KNOWN NAME NUMBER

2 You are energetic, strong, and artistic, but you need to work with a very large canvas to achieve good results. Be careful not to get bogged down in the details. Allow yourself to see the big picture.

COMPATIBLE LOVE PARTNER - 645
COMPATIBLE BUSINESS PARTNER - 867

Consider directing your ceaseless and abundant energy toward starting a family, Known Name Number 1.

KNOWN NAME NUMBER

3 You have a tremendous capacity to apply yourself, and you have the grit and determination to see things through. You can be a little too serious, though, and should learn to relax more.

COMPATIBLE LOVE PARTNER - 646
COMPATIBLE BUSINESS PARTNER - 868

KNOWN NAME NUMBER

4 You were sent here for a specific task, a purpose, a job. It's time you realized what that is and get on with it. You have been a rebel for too long now, and need to settle down and follow your true calling.

COMPATIBLE LOVE PARTNER - 647
COMPATIBLE BUSINESS PARTNER - 869

KNOWN NAME NUMBER

5 You have the drive and ambition, but may encounter setbacks. Could be that you have a slightly misguided approach. Perhaps you need to appear more serious in order to impress others.

COMPATIBLE LOVE PARTNER - 648
COMPATIBLE BUSINESS PARTNER - 861

KNOWN NAME NUMBER

6 Others see you as a bit ruthless, but those who know you well know that you are really very soft-hearted. You might do well to reveal this side of yourself to the people you meet, as well as to your close friends and lovers.

COMPATIBLE LOVE PARTNER - 649
COMPATIBLE BUSINESS PARTNER - 862

KNOWN NAME NUMBER

7 You came here to achieve success, and you have the talent and energy to do so. What seems to hold you back is a restless spirit, which makes you think you won't be happy. Be content with what you have.

COMPATIBLE LOVE PARTNER - 641
COMPATIBLE BUSINESS PARTNER - 863

KNOWN NAME NUMBER

8 Outside the home you are well liked and successful; but inside you tend to dominate a bit too much. Lighten up and relax. Take a load off. You don't have to be quite so much in charge. Learn to delegate.

COMPATIBLE LOVE PARTNER - 642
COMPATIBLE BUSINESS PARTNER - 864

KNOWN NAME NUMBER

9 Everything about you shouts determination and activity. You are so busy being busy you may well miss what it is you are attempting to achieve. Learn to stand back a step or two and see things from a distance.

COMPATIBLE LOVE PARTNER - 643
COMPATIBLE BUSINESS PARTNER - 865

BIRTH NUMBER
3
FULL NAME NUMBER
2

Those of you with a Birth Number of 3 are energetic and disciplined—depend on you to get the job done is what they all say. That's okay with you—you like a challenge. You even seek out difficult situations to navigate sometimes, just to keep yourself on your toes. It's a good thing you are seen as charming, as your Full Name Number of 2 tells us, or else you might just inspire some envy. Your Known Name Number below tells the other half of the story.

KNOWN NAME NUMBER

1 Keep on plugging away with your ideas. You may well be light years ahead of your time, but the world will catch up eventually, and you will achieve considerable success. Don't doubt yourself for a single second.

COMPATIBLE LOVE PARTNER - 654
COMPATIBLE BUSINESS PARTNER - 876

KNOWN NAME NUMBER

2 It is okay to love and be loved. You don't have to remain quite so aloof from the rest of humanity. Come on and get involved with the rest of us. You know you will like it, and deep down it is what you want.

COMPATIBLE LOVE PARTNER - 655
COMPATIBLE BUSINESS PARTNER - 877

KNOWN NAME NUMBER

3 By going your own way, you have achieved an awful lot, but there may come a time when you need a partner or two to help you. Time to learn how to work as part of a team. Start practicing now.

COMPATIBLE LOVE PARTNER - 656
COMPATIBLE BUSINESS PARTNER - 878

KNOWN NAME NUMBER

4 If you work steadily at everything you have set your heart on, dividends will be paid. Maybe not tomorrow, but eventually. Don't lose heart and don't lose sight of your vision. Know that you are right.

COMPATIBLE LOVE PARTNER - 657
COMPATIBLE BUSINESS PARTNER - 879

KNOWN NAME NUMBER

5 If only you could settle down and start concentrating on something—a new project, perhaps—you would benefit immensely. I know you like your easygoing attitude, but you aren't covering any new ground.

COMPATIBLE LOVE PARTNER - 658
COMPATIBLE BUSINESS PARTNER - 871

There is nothing like teamwork to get things done, Known Name Number 3. You'll soon find out that working with others can be fun.

KNOWN NAME NUMBER

6 You may find being out in the world a bit of a chore, but you have to get out of bed occasionally and search for fame and fortune. Contrary to your belief, it will not come looking for you. You enjoy talking about love.

COMPATIBLE LOVE PARTNER - 659
COMPATIBLE BUSINESS PARTNER - 872

KNOWN NAME NUMBER

7 You don't need luck; you already have talent and ambition. How did you end up with so many enviable qualities? It isn't fair—the rest of us are jealous. Try to look as if you have to work occasionally, will you?

COMPATIBLE LOVE PARTNER - 651
COMPATIBLE BUSINESS PARTNER - 873

KNOWN NAME NUMBER

8 You sweetly and quietly go your own way, and couldn't give a hoot about the dictates of convention, public approval, or peer group pressure. Good for you. I like your quiet but authoritative charm and drive.

COMPATIBLE LOVE PARTNER - 652
COMPATIBLE BUSINESS PARTNER - 874

KNOWN NAME NUMBER

9 Water will wear away a rock over time, and you have this same ability. You are relentless and determined, but you go about life in such a gentle way that people don't realize that you are as strong as steel.

COMPATIBLE LOVE PARTNER - 653
COMPATIBLE BUSINESS PARTNER - 875

Your Birth Number and Full Name Number are the same, which tells us that you are indeed how you seem to others: **strong, enthusiastic, optimistic, and tenacious.** The negative traits of the number 3—proud, controlling, and interfering—are also accentuated, however, so be careful, or you will make enemies. Your inner personality may show a different side of you altogether— perhaps a gentler one. Check your Known Name Number below to find out.

BIRTH NUMBER
3
3
FULL NAME NUMBER

It's time you faced your fears and confronted that which frightens you, Known Name Number 7. You will feel very relieved—and proud of yourself.

KNOWN NAME NUMBER

1 You have the talent, the energy, and the discipline to achieve anything you want. So why make such a fuss? We are all in awe of you anyway. You don't need to tell us how brilliant you are—we are well aware.

COMPATIBLE LOVE PARTNER - 664
COMPATIBLE BUSINESS PARTNER - 886

KNOWN NAME NUMBER

2 Although you think you work best alone, this isn't really true. At some point you will need to learn to trust, and to take a partner on board. This may well be your soul mate, although I know you don't believe in such things.

COMPATIBLE LOVE PARTNER - 665
COMPATIBLE BUSINESS PARTNER - 887

KNOWN NAME NUMBER

3 What can I say? You are everything we all yearn to be: successful, talented, well disciplined, and energetic. We look up to you as a calm and well-ordered role model. Don't let us down by hopping off the tracks.

COMPATIBLE LOVE PARTNER - 666
COMPATIBLE BUSINESS PARTNER - 888

KNOWN NAME NUMBER

4 Although you have a lot of talent and know where you are going, you also have a self-destruct button, which you love to press just as it looks as if you are about to become successful. Why do you do this?

COMPATIBLE LOVE PARTNER - 667
COMPATIBLE BUSINESS PARTNER - 889

KNOWN NAME NUMBER

5 If you delay or put off getting on with your life any longer because you are too busy having fun, you might just forget what it was you had set out to do. Don't lose sight of the goals you have set for yourself.

COMPATIBLE LOVE PARTNER - 668
COMPATIBLE BUSINESS PARTNER - 881

KNOWN NAME NUMBER

6 Why do you always doubt yourself? You know what you want to achieve is right, good, and proper. The world is waiting, so you might as well go for it now. Be careful; procrastination is the thief of time.

COMPATIBLE LOVE PARTNER - 669
COMPATIBLE BUSINESS PARTNER - 882

KNOWN NAME NUMBER

7 It's time to take the plunge. Just take a deep breath, feel the fear—and do it anyway. I know you're scared, but you will have to jump in sooner or later. It's best if you get it over with now, so you can relax. Go on.

COMPATIBLE LOVE PARTNER - 661
COMPATIBLE BUSINESS PARTNER -883

KNOWN NAME NUMBER

8 You know you're right. We probably think you're right. So why argue? Just get on with it, and stop wasting your breath trying to convince us that you are right. The results of your actions will speak volumes.

COMPATIBLE LOVE PARTNER - 662
COMPATIBLE BUSINESS PARTNER - 884

KNOWN NAME NUMBER

9 Every time you start out, you seem to get lost. Stop retracing your steps back to home base. You may flounder a little bit longer, but if you are determined, you will eventually see the light at the end of the tunnel.

COMPATIBLE LOVE PARTNER - 663
COMPATIBLE BUSINESS PARTNER - 885

BIRTH NUMBER 3

FULL NAME NUMBER 4

You do love to hear yourself speak, don't you, Birth Number 3? Your enormous reserves of energy are often spent chattering away, and it's apparent to all that you are brimming with self-confidence. We know from your Full Name Number of 4, however, that some see you as impatient and slightly opinionated. Your Known Name Number reading below can tell you a bit more about the real you.

KNOWN NAME NUMBER 1

You are a tower of strength. We all rely on you, and we all need you. That's fine, but you do need some comfort yourself, you know. If you don't learn to bend a little, you might find yourself breaking.

COMPATIBLE LOVE PARTNER - 674
COMPATIBLE BUSINESS PARTNER - 896

KNOWN NAME NUMBER 2

You are a rare creature indeed—a thoroughly nice person. There is not a single nasty bone in your body. You may be too good to be true—or just very good at hiding the bad stuff. Which one is it?

COMPATIBLE LOVE PARTNER - 675
COMPATIBLE BUSINESS PARTNER - 897

KNOWN NAME NUMBER 3

You have a vision. You have the support and love you need to accomplish your dream. You have the talent. So what holds you back, apart from this impish need to provoke authority? Stop it right now.

COMPATIBLE LOVE PARTNER - 676
COMPATIBLE BUSINESS PARTNER - 898

Delve deep into your inner psyche, Known Name Number 4, and try to figure out how such a sweet child grew into a cynical, jaded adult.

KNOWN NAME NUMBER 4

As a child you were a little sweetheart—full of good intentions and charm. Something happened to make you resentful and hard. Find the cause and you will find the cure. Go back and set things right.

COMPATIBLE LOVE PARTNER - 677
COMPATIBLE BUSINESS PARTNER - 899

KNOWN NAME NUMBER 5

Boy, are you having a whale of a time. You certainly seem to be having fun and getting everything you want out of life. Don't worry, the fun will continue for a long time to come. This is your enviable karma.

COMPATIBLE LOVE PARTNER - 678
COMPATIBLE BUSINESS PARTNER - 891

KNOWN NAME NUMBER 6

You devote a lot of time to your loved ones. Inside there is some resentment, though, as you would like more freedom. Wait a while and everything you want will come to you—and you won't have to sacrifice anything.

COMPATIBLE LOVE PARTNER - 679
COMPATIBLE BUSINESS PARTNER - 892

KNOWN NAME NUMBER 7

You have become trapped in a false world that simply isn't you. Break out now. This isn't what you set out to do and you know it. Listen to your intuition and go for your dream—not what everyone else expects of you.

COMPATIBLE LOVE PARTNER - 671
COMPATIBLE BUSINESS PARTNER - 893

KNOWN NAME NUMBER 8

What a trendsetter you are. There is nothing you don't do first—set the pace, defy convention, and give us all a wake-up call. But why the need to be so rebellious? You have nothing to prove—you are already impressive.

COMPATIBLE LOVE PARTNER - 672
COMPATIBLE BUSINESS PARTNER - 894

KNOWN NAME NUMBER 9

If there were a crisis, I would like you there to hold my hand. You have all the qualities of a great leader and are simply outstanding in emergency situations. You don't lose control and can see solutions instantly.

COMPATIBLE LOVE PARTNER - 673
COMPATIBLE BUSINESS PARTNER - 895

In ancient geometry, the number 3 is linked to the triangle, the symbol of logic, intellect, and reason. If 3 is your **Birth Number**, it may be fair to say that you are an inherently rational person, and are capable of making fair decisions. Your Full Name Number 5 tells you that others find you good company, and enjoy being around you. The Known Name Number reading below completes the picture of your personality.

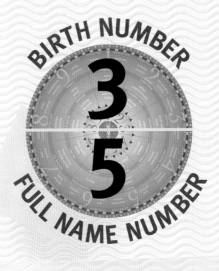

BIRTH NUMBER 3
FULL NAME NUMBER 5

KNOWN NAME NUMBER 1

Whoa! Slow down and rest for a while. You will burn yourself out if you don't take a day off. I know you need to keep busy to maintain your success rate, but you won't lose anything if you chill out occasionally.

COMPATIBLE LOVE PARTNER - 684
COMPATIBLE BUSINESS PARTNER - 816

KNOWN NAME NUMBER 2

By staying ahead of the game, you are doing rather well. If you start napping, though, the rest of us might just catch up. You are the hare and we are the tortoise. Stay on the move at all times—we're gaining on you.

COMPATIBLE LOVE PARTNER - 685
COMPATIBLE BUSINESS PARTNER - 817

KNOWN NAME NUMBER 3

There will come a time when you will need to settle down and find a partner—maybe even a job. Until then, enjoy yourself. Useless advice, I know, as that's the one thing you do superbly.

COMPATIBLE LOVE PARTNER - 686
COMPATIBLE BUSINESS PARTNER - 818

KNOWN NAME NUMBER 4

If there is a practical solution to the world's problems, you are the one who is talented and quick-thinking enough to come up with it. In the meantime, concentrate on more urgent matters closer to you.

COMPATIBLE LOVE PARTNER - 687
COMPATIBLE BUSINESS PARTNER - 819

KNOWN NAME NUMBER 5

You don't like being told what to do, nor do you like being given advice. Okay, I'll do neither. But you might want to listen to someone very close to you—they know what they are talking about.

COMPATIBLE LOVE PARTNER - 688
COMPATIBLE BUSINESS PARTNER - 811

KNOWN NAME NUMBER 6

You have a very gentle and pleasurable way of making your way through this world. You have an instinctive ability to know who to trust and what to do. Stay on the path that you are currently on and you will be just fine.

COMPATIBLE LOVE PARTNER - 689
COMPATIBLE BUSINESS PARTNER - 812

Don't let the world overtake you, Known Name Number 2. You are in the lead at the moment—do everything you can to make sure you stay that way.

KNOWN NAME NUMBER 7

I know the world is a fierce, frightening, gray place, and that you'd rather not be here. But you have to be here, so you must learn how to find light and color somehow. Try not to be so dreamy.

COMPATIBLE LOVE PARTNER - 681
COMPATIBLE BUSINESS PARTNER - 813

KNOWN NAME NUMBER 8

You are independent, entrepreneurial, and successful. But you are also difficult, bad-tempered, and rather controlling. You don't need these last three traits—try to concentrate more on the first three.

COMPATIBLE LOVE PARTNER - 682
COMPATIBLE BUSINESS PARTNER - 814

KNOWN NAME NUMBER 9

You have the discipline and the talent to be very successful. You also have the strength to upset the apple cart whenever you want to. Stop threatening, and either do it or back off.

COMPATIBLE LOVE PARTNER - 683
COMPATIBLE BUSINESS PARTNER - 815

BIRTH NUMBER
3
6
FULL NAME NUMBER

Typical of those with a Birth Number of 3, you enjoy a challenge, and love to be the one to come to the rescue when everyone is struggling with a seemingly insurmountable problem. No wonder people see you as reliable and trustworthy, if a bit unrealistic in pursuit of your lofty goals. You shouldn't be surprised that people think this—after all, your Full Name Number is 6. It might all be an act, though; check your Known Name Number below to find out.

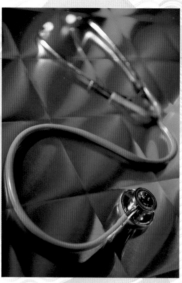

You can become a great healer, Known Name Number 7, if you use your remedial talents wisely.

KNOWN NAME NUMBER
1 Everyone around you knows how reliable and strong you are—but they may well be leaning on you just a bit too much. Learn to say no and mean it. I know you care for them all, but they are draining you.

COMPATIBLE LOVE PARTNER - 694

COMPATIBLE BUSINESS PARTNER - 826

KNOWN NAME NUMBER
2 Although you are successful and seem to have everything you want, there may be something missing from your life. Have you forgotten where it was you were going and gotten bogged down in the daily grind?

COMPATIBLE LOVE PARTNER - 695

COMPATIBLE BUSINESS PARTNER - 827

KNOWN NAME NUMBER
3 You have a marvelous talent for taking care of others, and you seem to genuinely enjoy doing so. Good for you. You may need to learn how to discharge all of that negative energy from others, though.

COMPATIBLE LOVE PARTNER - 696

COMPATIBLE BUSINESS PARTNER - 828

KNOWN NAME NUMBER
4 Sometimes we all have to compromise, if only to be able to work with others. This isn't giving in—it's being practical. You are efficient in every other respect, so why won't you just adapt yourself slightly?

COMPATIBLE LOVE PARTNER - 697

COMPATIBLE BUSINESS PARTNER - 829

KNOWN NAME NUMBER
5 Every time you feel the need to trust someone, do yourself a favor and allow yourself a bit of a cooling off period. You don't have to say yes to everything and everyone immediately—trust me, they will wait.

COMPATIBLE LOVE PARTNER - 698

COMPATIBLE BUSINESS PARTNER - 821

KNOWN NAME NUMBER
6 You have a great deal of energy, drive, and talent. They say it is being wasted on you, as you are too loving, too caring. Nonsense. Carry on exactly as you have been. You are doing all the right things.

COMPATIBLE LOVE PARTNER - 699

COMPATIBLE BUSINESS PARTNER - 822

KNOWN NAME NUMBER
7 You have a natural talent for knowing exactly what ails people. Use this talent well, and you will gain a reputation as a healer and counselor; use it unwisely, and people will see you as scheming and manipulative.

COMPATIBLE LOVE PARTNER - 691

COMPATIBLE BUSINESS PARTNER - 823

KNOWN NAME NUMBER
8 Bide your time before you react. Bite your tongue before you speak. You have a knack for being slightly too honest and forthright. The world isn't ready for such truth, and you could wind up hurting others' feelings.

COMPATIBLE LOVE PARTNER - 692

COMPATIBLE BUSINESS PARTNER - 824

KNOWN NAME NUMBER
9 My oh my what a determined person you are. You just don't give up. And why should you? Perhaps because you may be banging your head against a brick wall. On the other hand, you may find a breakthrough.

COMPATIBLE LOVE PARTNER - 693

COMPATIBLE BUSINESS PARTNER - 825

No one knows better than you how hard you have worked for your success, Birth Number 3. With your agile mind, you are truly gifted at overcoming obstacles. We know from your Full Name Number 7 that others recognize you as a very capable worker—that's why they always come to you for advice. But sometimes you wish that everyone would just leave you alone. Your Known Name Number reading below shows yet another side of your complex nature.

BIRTH NUMBER

3
7

FULL NAME NUMBER

KNOWN NAME NUMBER

1 Inside you there is all this desire, all this ambition. And yet you never quite seem able to get it out. Do you have the strength, but not the confidence? Do you have the drive, but not the follow up? Try a different approach and see if things improve.

COMPATIBLE LOVE PARTNER - 614
COMPATIBLE BUSINESS PARTNER - 836

KNOWN NAME NUMBER

2 If you follow the same old boring formula that everyone else uses, you are destined for failure. The world is finally ready for the wacky, the strange, the unorthodox, and the unconventional. And you are just the person to teach us.

COMPATIBLE LOVE PARTNER - 615
COMPATIBLE BUSINESS PARTNER - 837

KNOWN NAME NUMBER

3 You really must go your own way. You are being held back by too much advice, too many rules, and other people's opinions. Be true to yourself and you will really fly; listen to others and you will be grounded.

COMPATIBLE LOVE PARTNER - 616
COMPATIBLE BUSINESS PARTNER - 838

KNOWN NAME NUMBER

4 You have a natural talent for an intuitive approach to life. If you combine this talent with your ability to be real and practical, you will enjoy great success. If you are unrealistic, however, you will not get very far.

COMPATIBLE LOVE PARTNER - 617
COMPATIBLE BUSINESS PARTNER - 839

KNOWN NAME NUMBER

5 It doesn't all have to be so serious. Although you want to help, you can still enjoy what you are doing without it affecting you adversely. Lighten up and be happy about what you do.

COMPATIBLE LOVE PARTNER - 618
COMPATIBLE BUSINESS PARTNER - 831

KNOWN NAME NUMBER

6 Just because you love people doesn't mean they have to do what you tell them. Let them go free. If they return, it was meant to be. If they don't, it just wasn't. That's all there is to it.

COMPATIBLE LOVE PARTNER - 619
COMPATIBLE BUSINESS PARTNER - 832

Your luck may run out one day if you don't curb your dangerous ways, Known Name Number 9.

KNOWN NAME NUMBER

7 There is a nebulous energy inside you, a restless sprit that is trying desperately hard to get out. Let it out. Don't worry about what the world will think. You need to be the real you in order to thrive.

COMPATIBLE LOVE PARTNER - 611
COMPATIBLE BUSINESS PARTNER - 833

KNOWN NAME NUMBER

8 All your life you have been very individualistic and independent. This has always stood you in good stead, even if things have been hard along the way. Hang on to your ideals and don't compromise.

COMPATIBLE LOVE PARTNER - 612
COMPATIBLE BUSINESS PARTNER - 834

KNOWN NAME NUMBER

9 Be aware that much of what you dabble in has great danger for you. You are not invincible, nor are you immortal. It's time to consider others and stop pushing your luck—it cannot hold out indefinitely.

COMPATIBLE LOVE PARTNER - 613
COMPATIBLE BUSINESS PARTNER - 835

BIRTH NUMBER

3

8

FULL NAME NUMBER

People love working with you because you are enthusiastic, optimistic, and tenacious. The job will get done if it's given to you, Birth Number 3, no matter how busy you are. Others are tuned into your ability to focus and achieve your goals, and we know this because your Full Name Number is 8. But where does your drive and perseverance come from? Your Known Name Number reading below tells you about your inner personality, and may provide a clue.

KNOWN NAME NUMBER

1 Why are you reading this? You don't need to be. You already know that you are headed down the right path in life, and there is no doubt that you will reach your destination one day. Good for you.

COMPATIBLE LOVE PARTNER - 624
COMPATIBLE BUSINESS PARTNER - 846

KNOWN NAME NUMBER

2 It seems that you are being pulled in two directions. Part of you wants to be charming and pleasant, while the other part insists on being rude and belligerent. Which side will win? The choice is yours.

COMPATIBLE LOVE PARTNER - 625
COMPATIBLE BUSINESS PARTNER - 847

KNOWN NAME NUMBER

3 You can't always make people do what you want. They have to decide for themselves what to do, and if you badger them they will only resent you. Stand back and give them all some room to breathe.

COMPATIBLE LOVE PARTNER - 626
COMPATIBLE BUSINESS PARTNER - 848

You are a master of disguise, Known Name Number 5. You hide the real you very well—almost everyone is fooled.

KNOWN NAME NUMBER

4 Does the word rebellious mean anything to you? Of course it does. It is your middle name. There is no authority on earth that impresses you, frightens you, or makes you obey. But what about those not on earth?

COMPATIBLE LOVE PARTNER - 627
COMPATIBLE BUSINESS PARTNER - 849

KNOWN NAME NUMBER

5 You've been very lucky so far that no one has called your bluff. Can you keep it up indefinitely? I wonder. If you let the mask slip, even once, you will be done for. Aren't you tired of this endless charade?

COMPATIBLE LOVE PARTNER - 628
COMPATIBLE BUSINESS PARTNER - 841

KNOWN NAME NUMBER

6 You will only achieve true success when you can look in the mirror and be proud of yourself and what you've accomplished. Be careful not to hurt those who love you the most; be true to them and support them.

COMPATIBLE LOVE PARTNER - 629
COMPATIBLE BUSINESS PARTNER - 842

KNOWN NAME NUMBER

7 If you don't find a belief system to sustain you, things will only get worse. You need something to nurture you during darker times, and it will have to be something pretty unorthodox to satisfy you.

COMPATIBLE LOVE PARTNER - 621
COMPATIBLE BUSINESS PARTNER - 843

KNOWN NAME NUMBER

8 You have the discipline for hard work and successful relationships. You may lack a certain flair for diplomacy, but you can work on that. You may also be a little too intense, but that can be rectified—if you want it to be.

COMPATIBLE LOVE PARTNER - 622
COMPATIBLE BUSINESS PARTNER - 844

KNOWN NAME NUMBER

9 There is nothing that can stop you now. Keep the faith. Hold on tight to your dream and don't let anything stand in your way—and that means anything. Believe in yourself and your goals. You know that you are right.

COMPATIBLE LOVE PARTNER - 623
COMPATIBLE BUSINESS PARTNER - 845

Like most people with a Birth Number of 3, you may feel like a workhorse sometimes. But you wouldn't be so successful or wealthy if you didn't work so hard, right? From your Full Name Number 9, we know that others admire all the hard work you put into your charitable endeavors—and that the recipients really appreciate all you do for them. But there is more to you than this—look up your Known Name Number below to fill in the blanks.

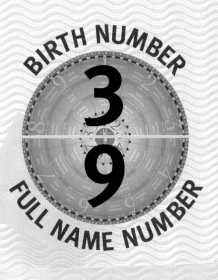

BIRTH NUMBER 3

FULL NAME NUMBER 9

KNOWN NAME NUMBER

1 You have the talent, the determination, and the strength to succeed. Now you have the permission as well. Follow your heart and stick to the truth. What more do you need? Oh, maybe a pat on the back. There, all done.

COMPATIBLE LOVE PARTNER - 634

COMPATIBLE BUSINESS PARTNER - 856

KNOWN NAME NUMBER

2 When you have something to say that actually means something to you, it might be best if you got someone else to say it for you. Otherwise, the message might get lost amidst the murder and mayhem that you cause.

COMPATIBLE LOVE PARTNER - 635

COMPATIBLE BUSINESS PARTNER - 857

KNOWN NAME NUMBER

3 What mysterious force drives you? You seem like such a nice person, and yet there is this dreadful need to take on the world. Back off and calm down. Breathe deeply. There, isn't that much better?

COMPATIBLE LOVE PARTNER - 636

COMPATIBLE BUSINESS PARTNER - 858

KNOWN NAME NUMBER

4 As I walk through the valley, I think I would like to have you with me. Is there nothing that frightens you? Bold and courageous soul that you are, you are never afraid, and you will never be beaten.

COMPATIBLE LOVE PARTNER - 637

COMPATIBLE BUSINESS PARTNER - 859

KNOWN NAME NUMBER

5 Your success in every aspect of your life—career, family relationships, romance—depends upon how much hard work you are prepared to put in. Oh, I see, very little. Well don't say you weren't warned.

COMPATIBLE LOVE PARTNER - 638

COMPATIBLE BUSINESS PARTNER - 851

KNOWN NAME NUMBER

6 You are successful, determined, and reliable. You are your own best friend and should listen to yourself more often. Stop prevaricating and follow your instincts. You may need to jettison some emotional baggage along the way, though.

COMPATIBLE LOVE PARTNER - 639

COMPATIBLE BUSINESS PARTNER - 852

Find a charitable cause or a spiritual system to believe in, Known Name Number 7, and dedicate yourself to it. You will be a much happier person for it.

KNOWN NAME NUMBER

7 If you channel all of that incredible energy into caring for others, you will go far indeed. But first, you need to find a cause that you think is worth championing, as well as something spiritual to believe in.

COMPATIBLE LOVE PARTNER - 631

COMPATIBLE BUSINESS PARTNER - 853

KNOWN NAME NUMBER

8 Go with the flow. You cannot turn the clock back, nor can you force the tide out when it is coming in. Learn to float downstream and enjoy the journey rather than struggling to swim against the current.

COMPATIBLE LOVE PARTNER - 632

COMPATIBLE BUSINESS PARTNER - 854

KNOWN NAME NUMBER

9 I won't upset you by telling you anything you don't want to hear—you are much too volatile for that. But I would advise you to take little bit of time out for relaxation before your pressure cooker blows sky high.

COMPATIBLE LOVE PARTNER - 633

COMPATIBLE BUSINESS PARTNER - 855

BIRTH NUMBER
4
1
FULL NAME NUMBER

You know deep down that you can be bombastic and opinionated, Birth Number 4, but you also know that this is part of your immense charm. You are lively and great fun to be around. These innate characteristics are perfectly compatible with your Full Name Number of 1, which tells us that others also see you as the life of the party. But there is more to you than just fun and games, and you know it. Your Known Name Number below can tell you what else there is.

KNOWN NAME NUMBER
1 You are a poor, driven soul, destined never to know any peace—that is, until you make it yourself, of course. But what then? Will you be able to relax? I doubt it. You are a hurricane of creativity, talent, and drive.
COMPATIBLE LOVE PARTNER - 744
COMPATIBLE BUSINESS PARTNER - 966

KNOWN NAME NUMBER
2 Keep at it—you are almost there. You have the necessary strength, drive, and determination to express yourself forcefully and extremely well. You may, however, need to curb some of your excesses.
COMPATIBLE LOVE PARTNER - 745
COMPATIBLE BUSINESS PARTNER - 967

KNOWN NAME NUMBER
3 By going your own way and sticking to your guns, you have a good chance of arriving at your destination. Don't compromise, just be a bit more diplomatic. You are disciplined and know your own mind.
COMPATIBLE LOVE PARTNER - 746
COMPATIBLE BUSINESS PARTNER - 968

KNOWN NAME NUMBER
4 You are headstrong and determined, and you know what you want to achieve. Perhaps you haven't quite learned how to get there yet, but your time will come—of that I have no doubt.
COMPATIBLE LOVE PARTNER - 747
COMPATIBLE BUSINESS PARTNER - 969

KNOWN NAME NUMBER
5 You are in great demand as an entertainer due to your enormous talent. You have charisma, and are fun to be around. Watch that temper, though, and easy on the sarcasm.
COMPATIBLE LOVE PARTNER - 748
COMPATIBLE BUSINESS PARTNER - 961

KNOWN NAME NUMBER
6 You seem to have found a new way to motivate people, and are very good at getting others to look at problems in a new way. This is a marvelous talent, and one you would do well to develop.
COMPATIBLE LOVE PARTNER - 749
COMPATIBLE BUSINESS PARTNER - 962

Your talent is renowned, Known Name Number 5. Audiences love watching you perform, and will travel great distances to see your shows.

KNOWN NAME NUMBER
7 No standard organized religion could ever hold any attraction for you. But a new cult? You may well become a founder or spiritual adviser of one. You are very unconventional, and don't mind rocking the boat.
COMPATIBLE LOVE PARTNER - 741
COMPATIBLE BUSINESS PARTNER - 963

KNOWN NAME NUMBER
8 There is an intensity and dark drive about you that people can find intimidating or scary. Lighten up a bit and allow people to see the friendlier side of your personality—we know it is lurking there somewhere.
COMPATIBLE LOVE PARTNER - 742
COMPATIBLE BUSINESS PARTNER - 964

KNOWN NAME NUMBER
9 There is nothing you will allow to stand in your way in your furtive race to the top. You have the courage, determination, and energy to overcome all of the odds against you. Stay the course—you'll be happy you did.
COMPATIBLE LOVE PARTNER - 743
COMPATIBLE BUSINESS PARTNER - 965

Others can always rely on you, Birth Number 4, and you cherish this reputation for steadfastness. You would do anything in your power not to let others down. Others see you as sensitive and intuitive, as we know from your Full Name Number 2, and frequently come to you for advice, especially in the romance department. But you are more than just a shoulder to lean on. Your Known Name Number below can tell you how much more.

BIRTH NUMBER
4
2
FULL NAME NUMBER

KNOWN NAME NUMBER

1 You have a wacky way of looking at the world, but with the right help and support, it will lead you to success and to great wealth. Use your unconventional thinking patterns to supplement your creativity.

COMPATIBLE LOVE PARTNER - 754
COMPATIBLE BUSINESS PARTNER - 976

KNOWN NAME NUMBER

2 One day you will suddenly understand how to operate in this world; you will clap your hand to your forehead and say "of course, it's so simple." Until then, you are destined to wander around in a state of confusion.

COMPATIBLE LOVE PARTNER - 755
COMPATIBLE BUSINESS PARTNER - 977

KNOWN NAME NUMBER

3 Just when everything is going well for you, you go and say or do something to upset it all. You have this terrible need to inflame or annoy others so that they withdraw their support. Next time, bite your tongue.

COMPATIBLE LOVE PARTNER - 756
COMPATIBLE BUSINESS PARTNER - 978

You used to question everything—and you made us do the same, Known Name Number 7. Lately, though, you have been asleep on the job. Wake up and be our guide again.

KNOWN NAME NUMBER

4 You are a charming revolutionary; a suave, sophisticated rebel who manages to incite revolution with kindness and gentle words. You have a way of getting people to question the world around them.

COMPATIBLE LOVE PARTNER - 757
COMPATIBLE BUSINESS PARTNER - 979

KNOWN NAME NUMBER

5 You have a talent for working skillfully with your hands to create objects of great beauty and usefulness. You might not yet recognize this talent, but you will soon—and so will every-one else.

COMPATIBLE LOVE PARTNER - 758
COMPATIBLE BUSINESS PARTNER - 971

KNOWN NAME NUMBER

6 When you find your soul mate, all of your dreams and goals will be fulfilled almost without you noticing. He or she will have nothing to do with it, it's just that you will be happy enough to aim for the moon.

COMPATIBLE LOVE PARTNER - 759
COMPATIBLE BUSINESS PARTNER - 972

KNOWN NAME NUMBER

7 You are here to make our lives uncomfortable, to make us question things and wake up a bit. The trouble is, it seems you have forgotten about this task and have fallen asleep as well. Who will wake you up?

COMPATIBLE LOVE PARTNER - 751
COMPATIBLE BUSINESS PARTNER - 973

KNOWN NAME NUMBER

8 There is an entire section of humanity you have chosen to ignore and cut away from your life. Why are you doing this? You are becoming isolated and reclusive, and are missing out on many things.

COMPATIBLE LOVE PARTNER - 752
COMPATIBLE BUSINESS PARTNER - 974

KNOWN NAME NUMBER

9 You seem determined to pick a fight. But who is brave enough to take you on? Perhaps only the universe itself. You are, of course, wasting your time. Better to pick on something a little less invincible.

COMPATIBLE LOVE PARTNER - 753
COMPATIBLE BUSINESS PARTNER - 975

BIRTH NUMBER 4

FULL NAME NUMBER 3

Nothing pleases you like a vacation to an exotic land, Birth Number 4. You are always up for an adventure, and value experiences far more than material possessions. Others recognize the free spirit in you—and how could they not? It oozes from every pore of your being! So your Full Name Number of 3 is in synch with your Birth Number. But there is still more to you to discover. Your Known Name Number below uncovers the rest.

KNOWN NAME NUMBER 1

You are steady, energetic, and strong. You work well, love deeply, and play hard. You are well balanced, if not a little too energetic and driven. But you are fundamentally good and wholesome.

COMPATIBLE LOVE PARTNER - 764
COMPATIBLE BUSINESS PARTNER - 986

KNOWN NAME NUMBER 2

Rebellious, successful, and charming are you. If you are not working in the entertainment industry, then you should be. You have a lot of talent and creative drive.

COMPATIBLE LOVE PARTNER - 765
COMPATIBLE BUSINESS PARTNER - 987

KNOWN NAME NUMBER 3

Apart from your need to be in charge—in control of every situation—you seem fine, if a little bit intense and independent. Perhaps you feel there is no one who understands you.

COMPATIBLE LOVE PARTNER - 766
COMPATIBLE BUSINESS PARTNER - 988

KNOWN NAME NUMBER 4

Don't expect success too early in life. Remember, when you are young and outspoken, people call you a rebel. When you are older and outspoken, people think you are a genius.

COMPATIBLE LOVE PARTNER - 767
COMPATIBLE BUSINESS PARTNER - 989

KNOWN NAME NUMBER 5

Pleasure seeking, rebellious, and independent—you lucky person. People envy and admire your unconventional lifestyle, and many would willingly trade places any time you wanted to settle down.

COMPATIBLE LOVE PARTNER - 768
COMPATIBLE BUSINESS PARTNER - 981

KNOWN NAME NUMBER 6

You have a fascinating and unique way of caring about people, and have the rare ability to really listen when they speak to you. You should keep honing this wonderful talent.

COMPATIBLE LOVE PARTNER - 769
COMPATIBLE BUSINESS PARTNER - 982

KNOWN NAME NUMBER 7

Allow others to walk their paths. Let them disagree with you. You may have found the right way for you, but understand that it is only one way. There is no right way—there are many ways.

COMPATIBLE LOVE PARTNER - 761
COMPATIBLE BUSINESS PARTNER - 983

KNOWN NAME NUMBER 8

Independence and individuality can be desirable qualities, but not if you start a fight with anyone who doesn't agree with you. Ease up a bit, stop being so defensive, and help others like you by being friendlier.

COMPATIBLE LOVE PARTNER - 762
COMPATIBLE BUSINESS PARTNER - 984

KNOWN NAME NUMBER 9

You have the drive to succeed, and you certainly have the talent, energy, and enthusiasm. The only thing holding you back is the need to find fault with everything everyone else does. You are something of a perfectionist. Ease up a bit.

COMPATIBLE LOVE PARTNER - 763
COMPATIBLE BUSINESS PARTNER - 985

Just because someone doesn't share your views doesn't mean you should instigate a fight, Known Name Number 8. Try to respect the opinions of others.

Number 4 is the sign of the earth, and the term "earthy" couldn't describe you better. Both your Birth and Full Name numbers are 4, which makes you about as grounded as it gets. Reliable and steadfast is how you would describe yourself, and you can be sure that others would agree. But you are so much more than just the rock that centers everybody's world. Your Known Name Number below explains just how much more.

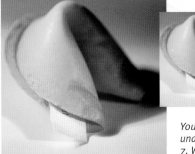
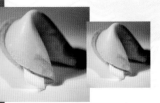

Your fantastic luck will continue unabated, Known Name Number 7. What great karma you have.

BIRTH NUMBER **4**
FULL NAME NUMBER **4**

KNOWN NAME NUMBER

1 You are direct, assertive, and energetic. There is certainly no doubt that you know exactly where you are going, how to get there, and what you are going to do when you arrive.

COMPATIBLE LOVE PARTNER - 774
COMPATIBLE BUSINESS PARTNER - 996

KNOWN NAME NUMBER

2 You are an artist, a creative genius who seeks recognition for your fabulous work. You'll get it, but only when you present it differently. You need to be more tactful and diplomatic.

COMPATIBLE LOVE PARTNER - 775
COMPATIBLE BUSINESS PARTNER - 997

KNOWN NAME NUMBER

3 You are very practical and enterprising. You are also independent, talented, and energetic. What more could you want? You seem to have found true happiness, and are very content with your life.

COMPATIBLE LOVE PARTNER - 776
COMPATIBLE BUSINESS PARTNER - 998

KNOWN NAME NUMBER

4 You have just about all the stamina, drive, ambition, and energy anyone in their right mind could possibly want. If you spend all that talent on yourself, you'll end up discontented. Spread it around.

COMPATIBLE LOVE PARTNER - 777
COMPATIBLE BUSINESS PARTNER - 999

KNOWN NAME NUMBER

5 All that energy and drive is being squandered and wasted. There's more to life than you think, but I'm not preaching. You must have a goal to strive for. Choose one and go for it, or you'll always regret it.

COMPATIBLE LOVE PARTNER - 778
COMPATIBLE BUSINESS PARTNER - 991

KNOWN NAME NUMBER

6 Deep down, you are soft-hearted, but you hide behind that cynical "I couldn't care less" manner. It doesn't fool anyone, though; we all know the real you. Give it up. Get honest with us and yourself.

COMPATIBLE LOVE PARTNER - 779
COMPATIBLE BUSINESS PARTNER - 992

KNOWN NAME NUMBER

7 You keep chancing your luck, and so far it has held out. But can it do so indefinitely? Knowing how audacious and crafty you are, the answer is probably yes. You must have one heck of a guardian angel.

COMPATIBLE LOVE PARTNER - 771
COMPATIBLE BUSINESS PARTNER - 993

KNOWN NAME NUMBER

8 You stand alone, head and shoulders above the present company you keep. The solution? Get a new set of comrades—find people who will understand and stimulate you. You are traveling in the wrong circles.

COMPATIBLE LOVE PARTNER - 772
COMPATIBLE BUSINESS PARTNER - 994

KNOWN NAME NUMBER

9 Everything about you says beware of danger, and the signals you send out scream "stay away!" Why is this? You have nothing to fear from us mortals. We only want to know and love you. Or is that the problem?

COMPATIBLE LOVE PARTNER - 773
COMPATIBLE BUSINESS PARTNER - 995

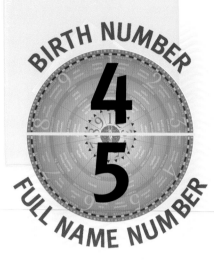

BIRTH NUMBER

4

5

FULL NAME NUMBER

You like spending time by yourself, Birth Number 4, but sometimes you feel like a hermit. You just need time alone periodically so that you can regroup and face the world again. You keep this private side of your nature to yourself most of the time, guarding it as you would a treasure. People know not to intrude, or so your Full Name Number of 5 suggests. Your Known Name Number reading below completes the mystery that is you.

KNOWN NAME NUMBER

1 You were born to be unconventional. You have achieved this in some measure, but you are still prey to what other people think. Time to go it alone and to stop worrying about public opinion.

COMPATIBLE LOVE PARTNER - 784
COMPATIBLE BUSINESS PARTNER - 916

KNOWN NAME NUMBER

2 If you settled down and got on with some hard work instead of wasting time on indulging all your passions, you could be very successful. Look to your dream and follow it through to completion.

COMPATIBLE LOVE PARTNER - 785
COMPATIBLE BUSINESS PARTNER - 917

KNOWN NAME NUMBER

3 You wasted a lot of time when you were younger, but you seem now to have discovered the secret of industry and diligence. Good for you. Success awaits you sooner than you think.

COMPATIBLE LOVE PARTNER - 786
COMPATIBLE BUSINESS PARTNER - 918

KNOWN NAME NUMBER

4 Bless you. You work away steadily and relentlessly, without any sign of recognition or praise. Why you should be so committed I don't know, but you deserve a day or two off—and a pat on the back.

COMPATIBLE LOVE PARTNER - 787
COMPATIBLE BUSINESS PARTNER - 919

KNOWN NAME NUMBER

5 Just because you have the means to enjoy yourself doesn't mean you have to constantly throw parties. There is a season for fun and a season for hard work. Looks like you may have skipped one.

COMPATIBLE LOVE PARTNER - 788
COMPATIBLE BUSINESS PARTNER - 911

You are in incurable and unabashed romantic, Known Name Number 7.

KNOWN NAME NUMBER

6 People rely on you, and you don't let them down. You accept your responsibilities gladly, with a cheerful smile on your face and a song in your heart. What makes you so happy? What's your secret?

COMPATIBLE LOVE PARTNER - 789
COMPATIBLE BUSINESS PARTNER - 912

KNOWN NAME NUMBER

7 You wear your heart on your sleeve. You love to be in love—and to tell everyone about how wonderful it is. But does it ever last? Is it ever as good as you think—and tell everyone—it is going to be?

COMPATIBLE LOVE PARTNER - 781
COMPATIBLE BUSINESS PARTNER - 913

KNOWN NAME NUMBER

8 You should learn how to take things a bit slower and steadier, as you have very low energy levels at times. But you are always optimistic, and are always up and eager to get on with the next project.

COMPATIBLE LOVE PARTNER - 782
COMPATIBLE BUSINESS PARTNER - 914

KNOWN NAME NUMBER

9 You can be very persuasive, and would make an excellent politician if you didn't think that such a job would be beneath your dignity. Oh yes, arrogance. That is another trait you have in abundance.

COMPATIBLE LOVE PARTNER - 783
COMPATIBLE BUSINESS PARTNER - 915

There is no more loyal friend than you, Birth Number 4. The trouble is, you don't always get the same degree of loyalty in return. You have been let down more than once, and it hurts. You can't help the way you are, though; soft-hearted and loving, you just can't turn away anyone in need, Full Name Number 6, and everyone knows it. But what you see isn't always what you get, as your Known Name Number reading below reveals.

BIRTH NUMBER 4

FULL NAME NUMBER 6

KNOWN NAME NUMBER 1

Stubborn, strong-willed, self-reliant, determined, obstinate—you name it, you've been called it. You can't be enticed out of your position by anyone once you've taken a stand. You are simply unmovable.

COMPATIBLE LOVE PARTNER - 794
COMPATIBLE BUSINESS PARTNER - 926

KNOWN NAME NUMBER 2

No one really understands you, do they? On the surface, you're very outgoing and confident; but underneath, you're a mass of complications and neuroses. You like going out, but not for long periods of time.

COMPATIBLE LOVE PARTNER - 795
COMPATIBLE BUSINESS PARTNER - 927

KNOWN NAME NUMBER 3

Those around you despair of ever seeing you sit down quietly for five minutes. You have others' best interests at heart and care deeply about those around you, but feel that none of this concern is ever returned.

COMPATIBLE LOVE PARTNER - 796
COMPATIBLE BUSINESS PARTNER - 928

KNOWN NAME NUMBER 4

If you don't allow a little time for yourself, you will suffer depression and stress-related disorders. Do yourself a service and learn how to say no. Shut the door and spend some time alone recuperating.

COMPATIBLE LOVE PARTNER - 797
COMPATIBLE BUSINESS PARTNER - 929

KNOWN NAME NUMBER 5

You are very compassionate, and are sensitive to the emotional needs of others. Why can't you pay the same amount of attention to your own needs? You can be quite moody due to the strain you put yourself under.

COMPATIBLE LOVE PARTNER - 798
COMPATIBLE BUSINESS PARTNER - 921

KNOWN NAME NUMBER 6

You have good taste and very expensive inclinations. You are well adjusted, know who you are, know what you are doing, and know where you are going. You have an abundance of confidence.

COMPATIBLE LOVE PARTNER - 799
COMPATIBLE BUSINESS PARTNER - 922

You certainly like the good things in life, Known Name Number 6. Precious jewels are a passion of yours, and you wear them well.

KNOWN NAME NUMBER 7

You are volatile, explosive, and intensely emotional. You have a great need to be loved, and can be very romantic. There is an unbending, stubborn side to you, but you can be warmhearted when you want to be.

COMPATIBLE LOVE PARTNER - 791
COMPATIBLE BUSINESS PARTNER - 923

KNOWN NAME NUMBER 8

There is something about you that is at odds with being in a romantic relationship. It could be that you simply refuse to compromise, but why should you if you like things the way they are? Maybe it's best if you stay single.

COMPATIBLE LOVE PARTNER - 792
COMPATIBLE BUSINESS PARTNER - 924

KNOWN NAME NUMBER 9

You don't fool me. You may fool most people around you, but not me. I can see that quivering heart, that restless, emotional plunge pool, that deep passion lurking beneath your cool, businesslike exterior.

COMPATIBLE LOVE PARTNER - 793
COMPATIBLE BUSINESS PARTNER - 925

BIRTH NUMBER
4

FULL NAME NUMBER
7

Luxury and indulgence are the two words that describe your ideal lifestyle, Birth Number 4. Hedonistic to the core, nothing pleases you like a trip to a health spa or a meal at a fine restaurant. Thankfully, the image you project to others is a bit more substantive; you come off as a spiritual, thoughtful person, Full Name Number 7, a good balance to your five-star desires. Your Known Name Number below completes the picture of your true personality.

KNOWN NAME NUMBER
1 Those around you, especially at work, think you are quick, efficient, organized, and very good at your job. And, indeed, you are; but under that coat of efficiency there is an untamed nakedness of hot lust and fiery passion.

COMPATIBLE LOVE PARTNER - 714
COMPATIBLE BUSINESS PARTNER - 936

KNOWN NAME NUMBER
2 On the surface, you are very moral and decent; but if we were to strip away the veneer, we might find a darker, more devious soul who longs to be cruel and vindictive.

COMPATIBLE LOVE PARTNER - 715
COMPATIBLE BUSINESS PARTNER - 937

KNOWN NAME NUMBER
3 You do have somewhat of a tendency to attract more lovers than any one person could safely handle, but somehow you seem to manage. Good for you, so long as you have the energy.

COMPATIBLE LOVE PARTNER - 716
COMPATIBLE BUSINESS PARTNER - 938

You flirt shamelessly, Known Name Number 3, but you're good at it.

KNOWN NAME NUMBER
4 You are dramatic, creative, and a virtual tower of strength to those who work with you. You have real talent, as well as a flair for organization and for putting on a show.

COMPATIBLE LOVE PARTNER - 717
COMPATIBLE BUSINESS PARTNER - 939

KNOWN NAME NUMBER
5 You can be quite solitary when you want to be. This can lead to problems in relationships, as others may not understand your need for space and privacy.

COMPATIBLE LOVE PARTNER - 718
COMPATIBLE BUSINESS PARTNER - 931

KNOWN NAME NUMBER
6 You are simply fantastic at picking and motivating a team to work with you. You will lead people to the very ends of the earth, and then make sure that they all get home safely.

COMPATIBLE LOVE PARTNER - 719
COMPATIBLE BUSINESS PARTNER - 932

KNOWN NAME NUMBER
7 You have inexhaustible supplies of energy and seem to be immune to sleep deprivation. You can be a bit intense sometimes, however, and need to learn how to sit back and relax a bit.

COMPATIBLE LOVE PARTNER - 711
COMPATIBLE BUSINESS PARTNER - 933

KNOWN NAME NUMBER
8 You find it extremely hard to make any emotional commitments, but you still expect your partners to make the same commitments to you. You often surprise people with this double standard.

COMPATIBLE LOVE PARTNER - 712
COMPATIBLE BUSINESS PARTNER - 934

KNOWN NAME NUMBER
9 You can be extremely stubborn at times, and like things to be done your way. Well, your way may be the right way after all. But have you ever considered that it may not be? Of course not. Good for you.

COMPATIBLE LOVE PARTNER - 713
COMPATIBLE BUSINESS PARTNER - 935

Although you pretend to enjoy spending time with your fellow human beings, Birth Number 4, the truth is that you'd rather be off on your own in an exotic locale. Trekking through mountains—solo, of course—is your ideal vacation. Your Full Name Number 8 tells us that others see this yearning for adventure as yet another one of your unconventional ways. Check the description of your Known Name Number for your inner personality reading.

BIRTH NUMBER 4
FULL NAME NUMBER 8

KNOWN NAME NUMBER
1 You are a contradictory, contrary soul with extreme mood swings and an almost impossible nature to fathom. You are intuitive, and use this power unwisely at times. You can be very demanding in relationships.
COMPATIBLE LOVE PARTNER - 724
COMPATIBLE BUSINESS PARTNER - 946

KNOWN NAME NUMBER
2 You are generous with your family, and enjoy giving them encouragement and support. If only you weren't so fussy and demanding. Leave them alone more often, and don't put so much pressure on them.
COMPATIBLE LOVE PARTNER - 725
COMPATIBLE BUSINESS PARTNER - 947

KNOWN NAME NUMBER
3 You are not one of the world's great leaders—good, we don't need any more—but you are an original thinker. You can be a little bit too independent, but why shouldn't you be?
COMPATIBLE LOVE PARTNER - 726
COMPATIBLE BUSINESS PARTNER - 948

KNOWN NAME NUMBER
4 You are very good at research and are interested in a variety of subjects. You like to quote facts in conversation, and have a highly retentive memory for dates and statistics.
COMPATIBLE LOVE PARTNER - 727
COMPATIBLE BUSINESS PARTNER - 949

KNOWN NAME NUMBER
5 It isn't laziness that describes you. It's just that you always see a flaw in the plan at the last minute—too hot, too cold, too far, too expensive...stop being so critical and get on with it.
COMPATIBLE LOVE PARTNER - 728
COMPATIBLE BUSINESS PARTNER - 941

KNOWN NAME NUMBER
6 You are one of the smartest people around, and yet you cannot stand back and see where your own faults lie. In your opinion, you don't have any. It's high time you admitted that you're not perfect.
COMPATIBLE LOVE PARTNER - 729
COMPATIBLE BUSINESS PARTNER -942

Your head is a veritable library of facts and figures, Known Name Number 4. You love learning new things, and accumulate knowledge quickly and easily.

KNOWN NAME NUMBER
7 You have an intuitive understanding of what people need to make their lives better—counseling, advice, help, support, and nurturing. People are precious to you, and you do everything in your power to help them.
COMPATIBLE LOVE PARTNER - 721
COMPATIBLE BUSINESS PARTNER - 943

KNOWN NAME NUMBER
8 You have limitless stamina, inexhaustible energy, and an adventurous, pioneering nature that keeps you outdoors much of the time. The wilder the weather, the happier you are. Better you than me.
COMPATIBLE LOVE PARTNER - 722
COMPATIBLE BUSINESS PARTNER - 944

KNOWN NAME NUMBER
9 You have everything you need: charm, good looks, vivacity, intelligence, and lots of love—but there is still something that refuses to let you join in completely. Perhaps you know something we don't.
COMPATIBLE LOVE PARTNER - 723
COMPATIBLE BUSINESS PARTNER - 945

BIRTH NUMBER

4

9

FULL NAME NUMBER

If you believe in something, you will defend it vigorously—a true sign of the Birth Number 4. You know this excessive loyalty to ideas or views can be annoying at times, but you can't help yourself. Some people find you hard to take, but others find you brilliant and inspirational, as we know from your Full Name Number 9, especially given your talent at communicating your ideas. Your Known Name Number reading below can tell you more about yourself.

KNOWN NAME NUMBER
1 You are extremely well adjusted, good at organizing both other people and yourself, work extremely well as part of a team, and are generally very adept at solving problems, both long term and short term.

COMPATIBLE LOVE PARTNER - 734

COMPATIBLE BUSINESS PARTNER - 956

KNOWN NAME NUMBER
2 You are one heck of a tough negotiator, with a very ruthless, dedicated streak. You work well within a team and are happy to take a back seat, but everyone at the meeting knows where the real power lies.

COMPATIBLE LOVE PARTNER - 735

COMPATIBLE BUSINESS PARTNER - 957

KNOWN NAME NUMBER
3 The world needs dreamers like you, or we would all be too serious and materialistic. You are a child of the universe, and are intuitively in touch with the heart and soul of humankind. You are also unrealistic and impractical.

COMPATIBLE LOVE PARTNER - 736

COMPATIBLE BUSINESS PARTNER - 958

KNOWN NAME NUMBER
4 You like egging others on to new and depraved experiences while you enjoy their discomfort and shame. You are the power behind the throne, but never the ruler yourself. Oh no, that would be too risky for you.

COMPATIBLE LOVE PARTNER - 737

COMPATIBLE BUSINESS PARTNER - 959

KNOWN NAME NUMBER
5 If you are not careful, your weaknesses will lead others astray. You enjoy seduction, and if the object of your lust happens to be in a relationship—well, so much the better. You are a romantic predator, and you know it.

COMPATIBLE LOVE PARTNER - 738

COMPATIBLE BUSINESS PARTNER - 951

KNOWN NAME NUMBER
6 You are an effective, hard worker who gets up early and enjoys being outside. You like to farm and grow things, and would like to find a way to combine your love of music with your love of farming and horticulture.

COMPATIBLE LOVE PARTNER - 739

COMPATIBLE BUSINESS PARTNER - 952

KNOWN NAME NUMBER
7 You are popular; but most people are a little wary of you, and you don't make friends very easily—acquaintances, yes, but real friends, not often. That said, there are a few people in your life who would do anything for you.

COMPATIBLE LOVE PARTNER - 731

COMPATIBLE BUSINESS PARTNER - 953

KNOWN NAME NUMBER
8 Whenever you feel settled and at peace, a tiny voice inside your head tells you that it is time to move on, time to be laying new tracks. Sometimes you want to shut the voice up and enjoy the peace and quiet, but you can't.

COMPATIBLE LOVE PARTNER - 732

COMPATIBLE BUSINESS PARTNER - 954

KNOWN NAME NUMBER
9 You have a lot to give the world and would probably be better off single. Not that this would ever happen, of course, as you need the dangerous cut and thrust of a relationship more than most of us do.

COMPATIBLE LOVE PARTNER - 733

COMPATIBLE BUSINESS PARTNER - 955

You are a real outdoors type, Known Name Number 6, and you feel confined if forced to spend long periods of time indoors.

You are a ray of sunshine in your friends' lives, Birth Number 5. With your wit and charm, people find you great company and a real joy to be around. And you are certainly no recluse—others see you as someone who loves going out into the world and having fun, as we know from your Full Name Number of 1. But are you having as much fun deep down inside as you seem to be having on the outside? Your Known Name Number below may provide a clue.

BIRTH NUMBER
5
1
FULL NAME NUMBER

KNOWN NAME NUMBER

1 You are a sensualist, a decadent pleasure seeker, and a very creative and active hedonist—and why not? You seem to enjoy life a great deal, and are capable of entertaining and amusing both yourself and others.

COMPATIBLE LOVE PARTNER - 844
COMPATIBLE BUSINESS PARTNER - 166

KNOWN NAME NUMBER

2 You can be very aloof, and might even be described as arrogant. I wouldn't dare, though. I will just say that you are superior and know it. You cannot fail to end up extremely wealthy—unless you get caught and go to prison.

COMPATIBLE LOVE PARTNER - 845
COMPATIBLE BUSINESS PARTNER - 167

You love the luxurious things in life, Known Name Numbers 1 and 3. Only the best foods, the finest wines, and the most expensive vacations will do for you—you just won't settle for anything less.

KNOWN NAME NUMBER

3 Make sure you earn a lot of money to cover your extravagance and generosity before you get into debt. You love entertaining, taking people out for meals, shopping, talking, being witty, socializing and generally spending money.

COMPATIBLE LOVE PARTNER - 846
COMPATIBLE BUSINESS PARTNER - 168

KNOWN NAME NUMBER

4 You are an ideas person, always ready to move on to the next project. The question is, do you ever finish anything? You are easily bored and like to change everything constantly.

COMPATIBLE LOVE PARTNER - 847
COMPATIBLE BUSINESS PARTNER - 169

KNOWN NAME NUMBER

5 When you find your soul mate, you will settle down and be very happy. Once you discover your career niche, you will be successful and wealthy. It's only a matter of time.

COMPATIBLE LOVE PARTNER - 848
COMPATIBLE BUSINESS PARTNER - 161

KNOWN NAME NUMBER

6 You have enormous talent and energy, but don't like to take any credit, except for a job well done by a cohesive team. You are a very supportive manager who gets the best out of people.

COMPATIBLE LOVE PARTNER - 849
COMPATIBLE BUSINESS PARTNER - 162

KNOWN NAME NUMBER

7 You are talented and often in demand as a problem-solver or troubleshooter. You have unlimited energy, which means that you can wear out those around you. You can be a bit much to take at times.

COMPATIBLE LOVE PARTNER - 841
COMPATIBLE BUSINESS PARTNER - 163

KNOWN NAME NUMBER

8 An innovator you most certainly are. You are very clever with your hands, and enjoy inventing and assembling new things. You have never been known to sit still, stay quiet, or be at a loss for an idea.

COMPATIBLE LOVE PARTNER - 842
COMPATIBLE BUSINESS PARTNER - 164

KNOWN NAME NUMBER

9 You might take care of others around you a little better and treat them a little more kindly. You tend to set exorbitantly high standards and then become very agitated if people cannot meet them.

COMPATIBLE LOVE PARTNER - 843
COMPATIBLE BUSINESS PARTNER - 165

BIRTH NUMBER

5
2

FULL NAME NUMBER

You have an uncanny ability to cheer people up, Birth Number 5, and it hardly takes any effort at all! Maybe it's your wacky sense of humor, or maybe it's just your zest for life. You'll be happy to know, as your Full Name Number 2 tells us, that others recognize that you can be emotional and sensitive, and that you need cheering up sometimes too. Check your Known Name Number reading below to find out about your inner personality.

KNOWN NAME NUMBER
1 Your reputation for calling a spade a spade can make people a little hesitant about asking your advice at times, as they know that you always tell the truth and never attempt to dress it up with flattery or restraint.

COMPATIBLE LOVE PARTNER - 854
COMPATIBLE BUSINESS PARTNER - 176

KNOWN NAME NUMBER
2 You have a genuinely caring and responsive nature, which enables you to work well with people without being needy. You can be a bit restless, and need lots of fresh air and exercise as well as intellectual stimulation.

COMPATIBLE LOVE PARTNER - 855
COMPATIBLE BUSINESS PARTNER - 177

KNOWN NAME NUMBER
3 You are happiest working in the arts, as this fulfills your enormous passion for art and expression. You do need to concentrate a bit more and gaze out of the window a bit less, however, and you could do with being a bit more focused.

COMPATIBLE LOVE PARTNER - 856
COMPATIBLE BUSINESS PARTNER - 178

Be careful not to let your gambling habit get out of hand, Known Name Number 4, or it could be your downfall.

KNOWN NAME NUMBER
4 You are a powerful force. People like being around you, as you radiate fun and warmth. You love to entertain at home—dinner parties are your specialty. You have a passion for gambling—keep it in check.

COMPATIBLE LOVE PARTNER - 857
COMPATIBLE BUSINESS PARTNER - 179

KNOWN NAME NUMBER
5 You can be stubborn and a bit old-fashioned, but you can also be very mellow and soppy when in love. You have quite a head for business and are extremely creative both inside and outside the workplace.

COMPATIBLE LOVE PARTNER - 858
COMPATIBLE BUSINESS PARTNER - 171

KNOWN NAME NUMBER
6 You handle responsibility well, but it is often thrust upon you unwillingly. But you don't let people down and are marvelous in a crisis—you don't panic or run away. You seek harmony and hate discord of any sort.

COMPATIBLE LOVE PARTNER - 859
COMPATIBLE BUSINESS PARTNER - 172

KNOWN NAME NUMBER
7 You are loyal and faithful to ideas as well as to friends. You usually maintain excellent health, are very robust, and enjoy being outdoors. You can be very jealous, but you are also forgiving and extremely kind.

COMPATIBLE LOVE PARTNER - 851
COMPATIBLE BUSINESS PARTNER - 173

KNOWN NAME NUMBER
8 You have a well-rounded personality, and are usually cheerful, with a sunny disposition. You typically wake up smiling and, if not upset about something, will maintain a cheerful frame of mind all day long.

COMPATIBLE LOVE PARTNER - 852
COMPATIBLE BUSINESS PARTNER - 174

KNOWN NAME NUMBER
9 You are a very trustworthy, reliable person, and you cope extremely well in emergencies. You are also very practical, and generally have no time to waste on what you would deem foolishness.

COMPATIBLE LOVE PARTNER - 853
COMPATIBLE BUSINESS PARTNER - 175

Change is a key word for you, Birth Number 5. You will experience many changes in your life; but have no fear, you will adapt easily to every one of them. You will never have any problem getting work if you change your living locale. Others see you as a hard worker, as your Full Name Number 3 tells us, so you will always be a valued employee. Your Known Name Number below can help you anticipate how you will react to all this change in your life.

BIRTH NUMBER 5
FULL NAME NUMBER 3

KNOWN NAME NUMBER

1 You can be very possessive and extremely jealous— often with no good cause. These traits can drive people away, which is what you fear most. You are a sort of self-fulfilling prophecy.

COMPATIBLE LOVE PARTNER - 864
COMPATIBLE BUSINESS PARTNER - 186

KNOWN NAME NUMBER

2 The dilettante of the artistic world, that's what you are. You may be seen as lazy, but you spend so much time creating that you don't have any time left to do anything else.

COMPATIBLE LOVE PARTNER - 865
COMPATIBLE BUSINESS PARTNER - 187

KNOWN NAME NUMBER

3 You can be tenacious, and have great vision. You set a goal and then work steadily and relentlessly towards it. You may have inherited some of your father's temper, which can be volcanic and unpredictable.

COMPATIBLE LOVE PARTNER - 866
COMPATIBLE BUSINESS PARTNER - 188

KNOWN NAME NUMBER

4 You are a born fighter: quick-tempered and rebellious. As you grow older, you will learn tact and diplomacy. Until then, those around you expect fireworks—and get them. Try channeling your energy into good works.

COMPATIBLE LOVE PARTNER - 867
COMPATIBLE BUSINESS PARTNER - 189

KNOWN NAME NUMBER

5 You could sell ice cream to Inuits. You work hard and know how to spend the results of your endeavors. You are a party animal, but then again, you are up and out there selling your wares at the crack of dawn.

COMPATIBLE LOVE PARTNER - 868
COMPATIBLE BUSINESS PARTNER - 181

Try to keep your fiery temper in check, Known Name Numbers 3 and 4. You will get far more accomplished if you behave in a calm and accommodating manner.

KNOWN NAME NUMBER

6 You are the great communicator of the numerology world. People listen to you, as you have great force and energy. But what is it that you have to say? Make sure it is worth listening to.

COMPATIBLE LOVE PARTNER - 869
COMPATIBLE BUSINESS PARTNER - 182

KNOWN NAME NUMBER

7 You have rare and mysterious magical powers —and you know it. Be careful to use these psychic abilities for good purposes lest they turn on you. You suffer from boredom and seek new challenges constantly.

COMPATIBLE LOVE PARTNER - 861
COMPATIBLE BUSINESS PARTNER - 183

KNOWN NAME NUMBER

8 The bull in the china shop—that's you. Always rushing into things without considering the long-term results. If you would only learn to control your impulsiveness and direct your energies more into team activities, you would fare much better.

COMPATIBLE LOVE PARTNER - 862
COMPATIBLE BUSINESS PARTNER - 184

KNOWN NAME NUMBER

9 Perhaps the world has grown too modern for such an old-fashioned character as you. You hold onto traditional values and refuse to move with the times —and why not? You believe in truth, honesty, and justice, and will fight for these values.

COMPATIBLE LOVE PARTNER - 863
COMPATIBLE BUSINESS PARTNER - 185

BIRTH NUMBER 5

FULL NAME NUMBER 4

You are certainly a smart one, Birth Number 5. You have a superior intellect and a gift for languages. For you, nothing beats a cup of coffee and a challenging puzzle. Others may see you as the nutty professor type, as we know from your Full Name Number of 4. You can be a bit of a slob, but that's only because material possessions don't matter to you. But do these characteristics really define you? See your Known Name Number reading below and find out.

KNOWN NAME NUMBER 1

Constant and true—that's you. You allow the world to see the real you—no hiding, no masks. Consequently, you are often surprised by how devious other people can be. You wear your heart on your sleeve.

COMPATIBLE LOVE PARTNER - 874
COMPATIBLE BUSINESS PARTNER - 196

KNOWN NAME NUMBER 2

You are strong, lively, and energetic—capable of exhausting those around you, but also capable of inspiring and motivating them. You have great stamina and can be very resourceful when you want to be.

COMPATIBLE LOVE PARTNER - 875
COMPATIBLE BUSINESS PARTNER - 197

KNOWN NAME NUMBER 3

You like to be a permanent fixture, hate change of any sort, and can be seen as stubborn or set in your ways because of this. This isn't necessarily the case; it's just that you like to be part of a tradition and a fixed set of values.

COMPATIBLE LOVE PARTNER - 876
COMPATIBLE BUSINESS PARTNER - 198

KNOWN NAME NUMBER 4

You aren't given to wild flights of fancy, daydreaming, or wanton longings. Instead, you prefer the safety and calm of your fireside chair, where you can pontificate on the world and all of its ills.

COMPATIBLE LOVE PARTNER - 877
COMPATIBLE BUSINESS PARTNER - 199

Only the best in life will do for you, Known Name Numbers 5, 6, 7, and 8. You have excellent taste and a discriminating eye.

KNOWN NAME NUMBER 5

You are stylish, educated, civilized, and very refined. You are also a bit of a snob, and love the fact that your breeding is of such high quality. Be careful, though, as you offend when you look down at "lesser folk."

COMPATIBLE LOVE PARTNER - 878
COMPATIBLE BUSINESS PARTNER - 191

KNOWN NAME NUMBER 6

You simply hate anything tacky, common, or garish, and are very discriminating when it comes to your clothes, your furniture, your house, your partners, and your life in general. You adore the good things in life.

COMPATIBLE LOVE PARTNER - 879
COMPATIBLE BUSINESS PARTNER - 192

KNOWN NAME NUMBER 7

You are a sensualist and are in love with the best that life has to offer, from food to clothing to music. You appreciate and admire beauty in art and literature, and have exclusive, exquisite taste.

COMPATIBLE LOVE PARTNER - 871
COMPATIBLE BUSINESS PARTNER - 193

KNOWN NAME NUMBER 8

The trappings of your life must be just right—homes, furnishings, cars, clothes, that sort of thing—or you will not be happy. You enjoy material success and comfort, and are prepared to work hard to achieve them.

COMPATIBLE LOVE PARTNER - 872
COMPATIBLE BUSINESS PARTNER - 194

KNOWN NAME NUMBER 9

You have a very inventive mind and are very clever. You are what might be termed an intellectual with very strong opinions, and you have a very forceful way of exploring the world around you.

COMPATIBLE LOVE PARTNER - 873
COMPATIBLE BUSINESS PARTNER - 195

Both your Birth Number and your Full Name Number are 5, which means what people see is what they get. Luckily, what they see and get are pretty pleasing: you are a charming, witty, cheerful companion, and are much loved by all, except when your temper flares, as it can do sometimes. If people bothered to look past your happy-go-lucky exterior, though, they might see more. Your Known Name Number reading below can tell you what that is.

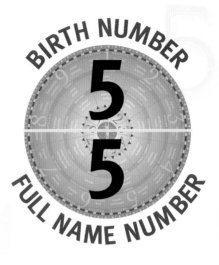

You are attracted to exotic destinations, Known Name Number 5. The only time you are truly happy is when you are off exploring the wild frontier.

KNOWN NAME NUMBER

1 You retain a youthful approach to life—always inquisitive, always ready to learn, and always inventive. You aren't judgmental of new ideas, and adapt quickly and easily to new technology.

COMPATIBLE LOVE PARTNER - 884
COMPATIBLE BUSINESS PARTNER - 116

KNOWN NAME NUMBER

2 Speed is your motto, and you often devise ways to save time, cut corners, and generally save work. You like results to be quick and efficient, and bring fresh energy and enthusiasm to any project.

COMPATIBLE LOVE PARTNER - 885
COMPATIBLE BUSINESS PARTNER - 117

KNOWN NAME NUMBER

3 You are a truly brilliant negotiator; you never let the other side see your true potential until it is too late and you have clinched the deal. This is why you are so successful in business—and so rich. Well done.

COMPATIBLE LOVE PARTNER - 886
COMPATIBLE BUSINESS PARTNER - 118

KNOWN NAME NUMBER

4 If you would stop talking so incessantly for just a moment, you would realize that there is no one left in the room listening to you. You have a thirst for adventure, excitement, and danger that frightens the rest of us.

COMPATIBLE LOVE PARTNER - 887
COMPATIBLE BUSINESS PARTNER - 119

KNOWN NAME NUMBER

5 The Ernest Hemingway of the astrological world— that's you. You are always seeking the next adventure, the next safari, the next escapade. And you are simply outstanding at recounting tales of your experiences, both orally and on paper.

COMPATIBLE LOVE PARTNER - 888
COMPATIBLE BUSINESS PARTNER -111

KNOWN NAME NUMBER

6 You have a big, emotional heart which yearns for love and companionship rather than grand passion and lust. You like to take center stage and be in the limelight, and people are drawn to you, as you have great personal magnetism and charisma.

COMPATIBLE LOVE PARTNER - 889
COMPATIBLE BUSINESS PARTNER - 112

KNOWN NAME NUMBER

7 Privacy is very important to you, and you can be quite shy and retiring at times. You are never at a loss for words, have limitless energy, and can keep going long after others drop.

COMPATIBLE LOVE PARTNER - 881
COMPATIBLE BUSINESS PARTNER - 113

KNOWN NAME NUMBER

8 You have a great talent for organization and make a good project co-ordinator. You can be a bit restless, and suffer from inner torment. You have a driving passion to change the world.

COMPATIBLE LOVE PARTNER - 882
COMPATIBLE BUSINESS PARTNER - 114

KNOWN NAME NUMBER

9 You like to have beauty around you and can be a bit snobbish about what you do. You tend to overrate your credentials; but what the heck, you have the charm to pull it off.

COMPATIBLE LOVE PARTNER - 883
COMPATIBLE BUSINESS PARTNER - 115

BIRTH NUMBER 5

FULL NAME NUMBER 6

You love a good crossword puzzle, don't you, Birth Number 5—anything to exercise your agile mind! You like to be challenged mentally on a regular basis. You can be quite anxious, but hide this side of yourself well; others see you as a lover of harmony, beauty, and balance, as we know from your Full Name Number of 6. You also keep other aspects of your inner personality well hidden. These are uncovered below in your Known Name Number reading.

It's time you realized that your aspirations to be Ruler of the Universe are a bit lofty, Known Name Number 9. Come join the rest of us down here on Earth.

KNOWN NAME NUMBER 1

Given enough time and trust, you can be as outgoing as the rest of us; it's just that you need to feel really secure and safe to venture forth. Once out, you are simply unstoppable.

COMPATIBLE LOVE PARTNER - 894
COMPATIBLE BUSINESS PARTNER - 126

KNOWN NAME NUMBER 3

You are a great lover of style, exquisite design, and décor. You enjoy perfect furniture arrangements and minimalist style. You can be found in large, clean, well-ordered white expanses of space.

COMPATIBLE LOVE PARTNER - 896
COMPATIBLE BUSINESS PARTNER - 128

KNOWN NAME NUMBER 2

You have many brilliant ideas, most of which involve making money by working from home. You may well become successful and wealthy without venturing outside your front door.

COMPATIBLE LOVE PARTNER - 895
COMPATIBLE BUSINESS PARTNER - 127

KNOWN NAME NUMBER 4

You have a tendency to panic when faced with adversity, and don't cope very well with bills or money management. But then, souls like you shouldn't have to.

COMPATIBLE LOVE PARTNER - 897
COMPATIBLE BUSINESS PARTNER - 129

KNOWN NAME NUMBER 5

Some people accuse you of being a bit of a dilettante, as you have never done a hard day's work in your life. Luckily for you, you don't care much about what others think of you.

COMPATIBLE LOVE PARTNER - 898
COMPATIBLE BUSINESS PARTNER - 121

KNOWN NAME NUMBER 6

You are very caring and warm, and you love helping other people. Don't let your negative side surface, though, or you might be tempted to use your skills and knowledge for evil ends.

COMPATIBLE LOVE PARTNER - 899
COMPATIBLE BUSINESS PARTNER - 122

KNOWN NAME NUMBER 7

You are friendly and charming, and are very good at putting people at ease. You don't have a particularly close family yourself, so you end up treating your clients and friends as your family. Lucky them.

COMPATIBLE LOVE PARTNER - 891
COMPATIBLE BUSINESS PARTNER - 123

KNOWN NAME NUMBER 8

You are a true individual of extremes—all black and white rather than shades of gray—and you make the rest of us look pale by comparison. You have a big, bright, and rather wonderful personality.

COMPATIBLE LOVE PARTNER - 892
COMPATIBLE BUSINESS PARTNER - 124

KNOWN NAME NUMBER 9

What you want to do is rule. To be the most senior, the most respected, the king or queen, the emperor, the Ultimate Ruler of the Universe. Heady ambitions, but let's be realistic; you may have to lower your sights.

COMPATIBLE LOVE PARTNER - 893
COMPATIBLE BUSINESS PARTNER - 125

You should watch your temper, Birth Number 5, or it may be your downfall one day. Luckily, you are quite cheerful and happy-go-lucky most of the time, especially when you force yourself to relax and have some fun. Because your Full Name Number is 7, we know that others take your bad temper in stride and chalk it up to eccentricity. But there is more going on in that formidable mind. Check your Known Name Number below to find out what that is.

BIRTH NUMBER **5**
FULL NAME NUMBER **7**

KNOWN NAME NUMBER 1

You are very secure in yourself, very self-reliant and balanced. You know where you are going and what you want to do. You are creative and extremely talented. You have never suffered a moment's self-doubt in your life.

COMPATIBLE LOVE PARTNER - 814
COMPATIBLE BUSINESS PARTNER - 136

KNOWN NAME NUMBER 2

You have a questioning brain, a sharp intelligence that borders on genius, and a natural ability to gather information and process it in a new and lateral way. Use this talent wisely and you will go far.

COMPATIBLE LOVE PARTNER - 815
COMPATIBLE BUSINESS PARTNER - 137

KNOWN NAME NUMBER 3

You are a flamboyant performance artist who likes to shock and horrify with your weird and wonderful tricks and your extraordinary talent for presentation. You are larger than life, and have great charisma.

COMPATIBLE LOVE PARTNER - 816
COMPATIBLE BUSINESS PARTNER - 138

KNOWN NAME NUMBER 4

You are often broke, drunk, and out of love. But what the heck, at least you know you are alive, and those around you know they are alive too because you help them, listen to them, and motivate them.

COMPATIBLE LOVE PARTNER - 817
COMPATIBLE BUSINESS PARTNER - 139

KNOWN NAME NUMBER 5

You are intelligent, witty, and a good communicator. Once you decide to change out of the somewhat tacky costume you presently seem to delight in wearing, you will be a force to be reckoned with.

COMPATIBLE LOVE PARTNER - 818
COMPATIBLE BUSINESS PARTNER -131

KNOWN NAME NUMBER 6

You are psychic and intuitive, interested in the soul and its fate, a lover of games and reading, and very fond of hugging and group work. You have a big heart and like to share your love. You are loyal and supportive, and make a good friend.

COMPATIBLE LOVE PARTNER - 819
COMPATIBLE BUSINESS PARTNER - 132

The next time you find yourself down on your luck, Known Name Number 4, take solace in knowing that you have many friends who admire you and rely on your steadfast allegiance to them.

KNOWN NAME NUMBER 7

You are never found at home if you can help it. You prefer to go out for fun, as your home is not really conducive to entertaining. You have a tenuous understanding of anything practical and can't even change a lightbulb.

COMPATIBLE LOVE PARTNER - 811
COMPATIBLE BUSINESS PARTNER - 133

KNOWN NAME NUMBER 8

There is an underlying impatience with people and a touch of arrogance about you, but you will need both to succeed where you are going. You love being in the spotlight and perform very well when in it.

COMPATIBLE LOVE PARTNER - 812
COMPATIBLE BUSINESS PARTNER - 134

KNOWN NAME NUMBER 9

You can be quite cold when it comes to love. This frigidity comes from your perceived need to protect yourself from being hurt. Perhaps it's time to lower your guard and start trusting others again.

COMPATIBLE LOVE PARTNER - 813
COMPATIBLE BUSINESS PARTNER - 135

BIRTH NUMBER

5
8

FULL NAME NUMBER

You are a master at correcting complicated situations. Truly, you have a real gift for overcoming adversity and bouncing back, Birth Number 5. Others see your ways as rebellious and unconventional, as we know from your Full Name Number of 8, but you know that there is no other way for you to be. You are just a natural troubleshooter. And there is more to you still. Your Known Name Number reading below reveals your inner identity.

KNOWN NAME NUMBER

1 You can be a little ruthless in your dealings with underlings, and have been known to be very rude to waiters. You like pomposity and old-fashioned standards. You may gain weight easily, but you carry it well.

COMPATIBLE LOVE PARTNER - 824
COMPATIBLE BUSINESS PARTNER - 146

KNOWN NAME NUMBER

2 Your greatest strength is the ability to see beyond the normal, the everyday, and the mundane, and you are able to pluck solutions out of the air that others would never have dreamed of. You are a real innovator.

COMPATIBLE LOVE PARTNER - 825
COMPATIBLE BUSINESS PARTNER - 147

KNOWN NAME NUMBER

3 You expect to be praised, adored, worshipped, and loved. If anyone even so much as thinks bad things about you, they are subject to your disapproval, and you often hold a grudge. Perhaps you should lighten up.

COMPATIBLE LOVE PARTNER - 826
COMPATIBLE BUSINESS PARTNER - 148

KNOWN NAME NUMBER

4 You love exploring the darker recesses of the human soul, and experimenting with varied modes of spirituality. You are warm and funny as well, although you have been known to take yourself very seriously.

COMPATIBLE LOVE PARTNER - 827
COMPATIBLE BUSINESS PARTNER - 149

KNOWN NAME NUMBER

5 You can be emotionally needy, but if you receive a lot of reassurance, you are satisfied. You can handle hard work and long hours, just so long as you don't have to go out and talk to a lot of people.

COMPATIBLE LOVE PARTNER - 828
COMPATIBLE BUSINESS PARTNER - 141

KNOWN NAME NUMBER

6 You often display a remarkable aptitude for disguises, and frequently people who know you well fail to recognize you. You like to change your personal appearance quite often to keep things interesting.

COMPATIBLE LOVE PARTNER - 829
COMPATIBLE BUSINESS PARTNER - 142

Money rules your world, Known Name Number 9. Just be careful not to become a slave to it.

KNOWN NAME NUMBER

7 You are always available, yet you are always in demand and are constantly busy. You like it like this, and can become miserable and sulky when left alone or when you don't have enough work to do.

COMPATIBLE LOVE PARTNER - 821
COMPATIBLE BUSINESS PARTNER - 143

KNOWN NAME NUMBER

8 You have a very easy way about you that impresses people, and they are very likely to trust you. You are a good lover, although you do tend to pick partners who may be of some use to you.

COMPATIBLE LOVE PARTNER - 822
COMPATIBLE BUSINESS PARTNER - 144

KNOWN NAME NUMBER

9 You are motivated by money, but not by power or prestige. You like money for the comforts it can provide and the luxuries it can buy. It's lucky that you have the talent, drive, and connections to make lots of it.

COMPATIBLE LOVE PARTNER - 823
COMPATIBLE BUSINESS PARTNER - 145

You need to be very careful not to find yourself stuck in a rut—either in work, play, or love—as this can be very dangerous for you, Birth Number 5. You do a good job of projecting a different you to the outside world, though: intense, energetic, and a lover of excitement is how others see you, as we know from your Full Name Number of 9. In all probability, the real you lies somewhere in between. See your Known Name Number below to find out more.

BIRTH NUMBER 5
FULL NAME NUMBER 9

You take very good care of yourself, Known Name Number 6, and it shows.

KNOWN NAME NUMBER 1

What you need is something solid, tangible, and practical to keep you organized. A decent Filofax or a laptop computer will do just fine. You take your work seriously, and don't have a lot of time for socializing.

COMPATIBLE LOVE PARTNER - 834

COMPATIBLE BUSINESS PARTNER - 156

KNOWN NAME NUMBER 2

Everything in your life is planned down to the very last detail. You leave nothing to chance, and simply hate surprises and the unexpected. You enjoy the cut and thrust of business and like it when negotiations go your way.

COMPATIBLE LOVE PARTNER - 835

COMPATIBLE BUSINESS PARTNER - 157

KNOWN NAME NUMBER 3

Although you have a very soft heart, you believe that people should make their own way in the world, and think that too much help makes people weak. You also think that most people are in need of motivation.

COMPATIBLE LOVE PARTNER - 836

COMPATIBLE BUSINESS PARTNER - 158

KNOWN NAME NUMBER 4

You are forceful and strong, courageous and daring, reckless at times, and domineering and dominant. You will be a strong, proud leader in whichever career you decide on—most likely as the head of a company.

COMPATIBLE LOVE PARTNER - 837

COMPATIBLE BUSINESS PARTNER - 159

KNOWN NAME NUMBER 5

You are very independent, but might like to work more with a team to help you shoulder some of the responsibility. You have very refined taste, and can be a little old-fashioned and reactionary in some situations.

COMPATIBLE LOVE PARTNER - 838

COMPATIBLE BUSINESS PARTNER - 151

KNOWN NAME NUMBER 6

According to you, there is one rule for us and another for yourself, if you know what I mean. You are very attractive and like to stay looking young and healthy. Looking successful and fit is very important to you.

COMPATIBLE LOVE PARTNER - 839

COMPATIBLE BUSINESS PARTNER - 152

KNOWN NAME NUMBER 7

Stylish and attractive are words that describe you well. You are very much in demand as a social humorist and raconteur. You love nothing better than to play the part of the amusing wit at sophisticated dinner parties.

COMPATIBLE LOVE PARTNER - 831

COMPATIBLE BUSINESS PARTNER - 153

KNOWN NAME NUMBER 8

You are a mechanical genius, but you are also a grumpy nitpicker who expects perfection and seriousness in everything. You can be a bit taciturn, and haven't much time for entertainment or foolishness.

COMPATIBLE LOVE PARTNER - 832

COMPATIBLE BUSINESS PARTNER - 154

KNOWN NAME NUMBER 9

Life should be peaceful and full of beauty, you think. You see no reason why you should have to look at or take part in the seamier side of life. Your existence is built around refinement, charm, style, and elegance.

COMPATIBLE LOVE PARTNER - 833

COMPATIBLE BUSINESS PARTNER - 155

BIRTH NUMBER

6

1

FULL NAME NUMBER

Those of you with a Birth Number of 6 tend to be reliable and trustworthy. Your idea of a perfect day is one spent peacefully at home, perhaps in your yard, relaxing and hanging out with your family. Others see you as honest and upright, as we can see from your Full Name Number of 1. But there are other, more complicated sides to you too. Look at your Known Name Number reading below to find out what these are.

KNOWN NAME NUMBER

1 You can be quick-tempered, impulsive, and impatient—you want everything now. You are also enthusiastic and generous, and very quick-thinking in emergencies.

COMPATIBLE LOVE PARTNER - 944
COMPATIBLE BUSINESS PARTNER - 266

KNOWN NAME NUMBER

2 You are not so hung up about looks; you are more concerned with principles, morals, and fortitude. You are very practical and clever with your hands, and can fix almost anything in a pinch.

COMPATIBLE LOVE PARTNER - 945
COMPATIBLE BUSINESS PARTNER - 267

KNOWN NAME NUMBER

3 You can be conservative in your outlook, and aren't too ready to try new things; you prefer old, well-established ways and methods. You like to look ahead and to plan carefully.

COMPATIBLE LOVE PARTNER - 946
COMPATIBLE BUSINESS PARTNER - 268

The inner workings of everyday items fascinate you, Known Name Number 2, and you understand how they function. This is why you are so good at repair work.

KNOWN NAME NUMBER

4 When you have something to say you speak up, but you can be quite silent the rest of the time. You think deeply about things, and don't rush to conclusions or make assumptions. You are easily embarrassed and detest anything risqué or smutty.

COMPATIBLE LOVE PARTNER - 947
COMPATIBLE BUSINESS PARTNER - 269

KNOWN NAME NUMBER

5 You are a bit of a secret prude, and are prone to getting stuck in ruts. Friends look up to you, and know they can rely on you. You don't like having fun made at your expense, and are slow to anger. When you do blow, though, you do it in style.

COMPATIBLE LOVE PARTNER - 948
COMPATIBLE BUSINESS PARTNER - 261

KNOWN NAME NUMBER

6 You can be prone to clumsiness if you try to move quicker than you want to—which is usually quite slowly. Some see you as stubborn. You like to be comfortable, and will save money to make sure you won't have to go without later in life.

COMPATIBLE LOVE PARTNER - 949
COMPATIBLE BUSINESS PARTNER - 262

KNOWN NAME NUMBER

7 You are an old-fashioned lover who expects roles to be observed and traditions to be kept. The whole business of seduction and flirting is not for you. When you do fall in love, there will be a proper courtship.

COMPATIBLE LOVE PARTNER - 941
COMPATIBLE BUSINESS PARTNER - 263

KNOWN NAME NUMBER

8 You are an excellent judge of character, so you usually choose your partners well. When you do make a mistake, though, nobody can convince you of it, and you will put up with a lot rather than admit you were wrong.

COMPATIBLE LOVE PARTNER - 942
COMPATIBLE BUSINESS PARTNER - 264

KNOWN NAME NUMBER

9 You have limitless patience and are extremely affectionate with your offspring. You aren't much for playing games, preferring a more educational approach; but children will always thrive under your care.

COMPATIBLE LOVE PARTNER - 943
COMPATIBLE BUSINESS PARTNER - 265

The number 6 signifies harmony, beauty, balance, and perfection. Those of you with 6 as your Birth Number are attuned to each of these qualities, and they influence your life in significant ways. Other people see you as more concerned with emotions than actions, as we know from your Full Name Number of 2. This makes you seem sensitive and charming. Your Known Name Number below rounds out the full picture of your personality.

BIRTH NUMBER
6
2
FULL NAME NUMBER

KNOWN NAME NUMBER

1 You tend to put on weight, owing to all that good food you like; but you carry it well. You are not great at expressing your emotions, but you can become depressed if you bottle them up. Learn to talk about how you feel.

COMPATIBLE LOVE PARTNER - 954
COMPATIBLE BUSINESS PARTNER - 276

KNOWN NAME NUMBER

2 Your love of good food knows no limits. You are an excellent cook and love to show off your culinary skills. The food you cook is heavy, filling, and traditional—no contemporary cuisine is made in your home.

COMPATIBLE LOVE PARTNER - 955
COMPATIBLE BUSINESS PARTNER - 277

KNOWN NAME NUMBER

3 You have strong opinions, which you will defend until the end—or until you decide to change them. You can be extremely amusing and talkative, and have a great flair for languages and communication.

COMPATIBLE LOVE PARTNER - 956
COMPATIBLE BUSINESS PARTNER - 278

KNOWN NAME NUMBER

4 You are a quick-thinking, independent sort of person who likes to be out in the world, wheeling and dealing and talking a lot. You can sell anything to anybody, and enjoy the challenge of a difficult prospect.

COMPATIBLE LOVE PARTNER - 957
COMPATIBLE BUSINESS PARTNER - 279

KNOWN NAME NUMBER

5 If you can't learn it instantly, you claim you don't want to know it. You don't like being beaten by anything, but you also don't like to have to concentrate for too long. You are limiting your horizons.

COMPATIBLE LOVE PARTNER - 958
COMPATIBLE BUSINESS PARTNER - 271

KNOWN NAME NUMBER

6 You are a romantic idealist and expect your partner to be the same. It is often you that gets hurt in love affairs rather than the other person, and you some-times find yourself overwhelmed by conflicting emotions when you are in love.

COMPATIBLE LOVE PARTNER - 959
COMPATIBLE BUSINESS PARTNER - 272

KNOWN NAME NUMBER

7 You expect everything to be perfect and are very disappointed when it is not. Sometimes you don't think before you speak, and you find yourself promising a great deal more than you can successfully commit to or deliver.

COMPATIBLE LOVE PARTNER - 951
COMPATIBLE BUSINESS PARTNER - 273

KNOWN NAME NUMBER

8 You have a drive and intensity that can be so focused and energetic that it can be scary. All that pent up emotion is released, and you really go for it. You are old-fashioned in the sense that you equate sex with love and expect the same of your lover.

COMPATIBLE LOVE PARTNER - 952
COMPATIBLE BUSINESS PARTNER - 274

KNOWN NAME NUMBER

9 You are simply outstanding at getting information across quickly and succinctly. You talk fast, learn rapidly, and communicate extremely well. You are also very charismatic, and are a natural showperson, presenter, and salesperson.

COMPATIBLE LOVE PARTNER - 953
COMPATIBLE BUSINESS PARTNER - 275

Your idea of the perfect evening, Known Name Numbers 1 and 2, involves a witty and entertaining dinner partner, a scrumptious meal, fine wine, and a delicious dessert.

BIRTH NUMBER
6
3
FULL NAME NUMBER

You are often accused of being too soft-hearted, Birth Number 6, but that's just the way you are—tough and cynical you are not. You project an energetic, disciplined image to others, as we know from your Full Name Number of 3, and everyone knows that you get things done. But you are a more complicated being than this—one might even say that you are not what you seem. Check your Known Name Number below to get in touch with your hidden side.

KNOWN NAME NUMBER

1 You don't respond well to authority, and thus it makes sense for you to work for yourself. The daily grind of an office routine will drive you mad, so get out there and sell your goods—it's what you're best at.

COMPATIBLE LOVE PARTNER - 964
COMPATIBLE BUSINESS PARTNER - 286

KNOWN NAME NUMBER

3 Savings are not something you even think about—live for today, that's you. You'll be miserable in your old age if you don't put something away now. Seek out an occupation that uses your natural talents.

COMPATIBLE LOVE PARTNER - 965
COMPATIBLE BUSINESS PARTNER - 287

You love children and they adore you, Known Name Number 6. You are destined to be a great parent.

KNOWN NAME NUMBER

2 Like everything you do, your social life is frenetic and busy—there are lots of people you are close to and love talking to. The more activity and fast cars, fast foods, and fast adventures in your life, the happier you are.

COMPATIBLE LOVE PARTNER - 966
COMPATIBLE BUSINESS PARTNER - 288

KNOWN NAME NUMBER

4 You have a few really good friends, but friendships are something that let you down often. No one gives as much as you do and, consequently, you are sometimes hurt by other people's indifference or lack of commitment.

COMPATIBLE LOVE PARTNER - 967
COMPATIBLE BUSINESS PARTNER - 289

KNOWN NAME NUMBER

5 You suffer from a fear that you are missing something, and you are quite right. You rush everywhere and everything. In this way you miss a lot, as you are always between things—never where the action really is.

COMPATIBLE LOVE PARTNER - 968
COMPATIBLE BUSINESS PARTNER - 281

KNOWN NAME NUMBER

6 You can be very emotional and overly sensitive sometimes, but you are basically sympathetic and kind. You have a strong maternal instinct and a powerful imagination. Your feelings run very deep.

COMPATIBLE LOVE PARTNER - 969
COMPATIBLE BUSINESS PARTNER - 282

KNOWN NAME NUMBER

7 You love to dress comfortably—anything old and well-loved will do, as long as you feel comfortable in it. You aren't a great follower of fashion; although when you were younger, you may have gone through a period of rebellion.

COMPATIBLE LOVE PARTNER - 961
COMPATIBLE BUSINESS PARTNER - 283

KNOWN NAME NUMBER

8 You are shrewd and clever, with a very strong intuitive power that stems from your knowledge of feelings and where they come from. You would make a very good counselor. You can, however, be a bit too sensitive, and will remember an insult forever.

COMPATIBLE LOVE PARTNER - 962
COMPATIBLE BUSINESS PARTNER - 284

KNOWN NAME NUMBER

9 You don't forgive very easily if you've been wronged. You understand and are aware of the emotions of others, and you use this knowledge sometimes for manipulative purposes. You are very possessive; learn how to relinquish some control.

COMPATIBLE LOVE PARTNER - 963
COMPATIBLE BUSINESS PARTNER - 285

If there is a stray animal in the neighborhood it will find a home with you, Birth Number 6. You don't have the heart to refuse any living being in need, and often play the role of savior. This charitable aspect of your personality doesn't stop you from having a good time, however, and everyone knows you love to indulge yourself; your Full Name Number of 4 tells us this. Check your Known Name Number below to find out what else you are capable of.

BIRTH NUMBER
6
4
FULL NAME NUMBER

KNOWN NAME NUMBER
1 You love your family, and anyone else who loves them as much as you do. You are also fiercely protective of them. You don't, however, like to be criticized or confronted by your family—or by anyone else.
COMPATIBLE LOVE PARTNER - 974
COMPATIBLE BUSINESS PARTNER - 296

KNOWN NAME NUMBER
2 You expect to be in charge, and can stifle relationships if you're not careful through your need to explore and express your feelings in depth. Give your loved ones some room to breathe and things will be better. You'll see.
COMPATIBLE LOVE PARTNER - 975
COMPATIBLE BUSINESS PARTNER - 297

KNOWN NAME NUMBER
3 You are a great romantic and expect to fall in love forever at first sight, which you frequently do. You love to be wined and dined, and spoiled with presents, outings, and romantic evenings in front of the fire.
COMPATIBLE LOVE PARTNER - 976
COMPATIBLE BUSINESS PARTNER - 298

When you fall in love, you fall hard, and expect it to last for all eternity. You are a hopeless romantic, Known Name Number 3, but that is what makes you so charming.

KNOWN NAME NUMBER
4 If treated respectfully in love, you respond well and are a steadfast and faithful companion. If you are treated badly, however, you retreat into an emotional shell and it's impossible to get you to come out again.
COMPATIBLE LOVE PARTNER - 977
COMPATIBLE BUSINESS PARTNER - 299

KNOWN NAME NUMBER
5 You shoulder responsibility well, and make a very industrious and well-behaved employee. Any supervisor you ever have will feel completely confident about leaving you on your own to complete a project.
COMPATIBLE LOVE PARTNER - 978
COMPATIBLE BUSINESS PARTNER - 291

KNOWN NAME NUMBER
6 As an employer, you are good at motivating your staff, although you set very high standards and take it personally if they are not met. You really ought to work from home, though, as that is where you are happiest.
COMPATIBLE LOVE PARTNER - 979
COMPATIBLE BUSINESS PARTNER - 292

KNOWN NAME NUMBER
7 If there's anything you really like doing, it is socializing with your very close friends. You like to look after them, and this means feeding them, buying presents for them, remembering them, phoning them, and being concerned with their health and welfare.
COMPATIBLE LOVE PARTNER - 971
COMPATIBLE BUSINESS PARTNER - 293

KNOWN NAME NUMBER
8 You are likely to put a lot of time into your home and yard, and prefer to spend your time there rather than out in the wide world. You have a strong interest in consumer affairs and world politics, and often champion the cause of the underdog.
COMPATIBLE LOVE PARTNER - 972
COMPATIBLE BUSINESS PARTNER - 294

KNOWN NAME NUMBER
9 You have a wonderful imagination, and can turn a hovel into a palace overnight. You are neat to the point of obsession, though, and this can stop your friends from relaxing in your home as much as they might like to.
COMPATIBLE LOVE PARTNER - 973
COMPATIBLE BUSINESS PARTNER - 295

BIRTH NUMBER
6
5
FULL NAME NUMBER

It must be said that sometimes you have your head in the clouds, Birth Number 6. You mean so well and try so hard, but you are utterly unrealistic and impractical, especially in your quest to end poverty and suffering. Luckily, your earnestness is tempered by your sense of humor, and others just can't get enough—you really are the life of the party, Full Name Number 5. Yet there is more to you than meets the eye, as your Known Name Number below shows us.

KNOWN NAME NUMBER
1 You are creative and enthusiastic, energetic and positive. You are a bit dramatic and attention seeking at times, but you certainly have the talent, charm, and personality to be at the very forefront of most things.
COMPATIBLE LOVE PARTNER - 984
COMPATIBLE BUSINESS PARTNER - 216

KNOWN NAME NUMBER
2 You live off your charisma and charm, and the way you dress exudes these qualities. You are stylish, fashionable, well groomed, sleek, and sophisticated. Nice clothes are a religion for you. People look to you for fashion tips.
COMPATIBLE LOVE PARTNER - 985
COMPATIBLE BUSINESS PARTNER - 217

KNOWN NAME NUMBER
3 You are among the most cheerful of people. You greet misfortune with open arms, as it gives you the opportunity to display your remarkable powers of recovery.
COMPATIBLE LOVE PARTNER - 986
COMPATIBLE BUSINESS PARTNER - 218

KNOWN NAME NUMBER
4 You are extremely generous with your time, hospitality, and friendships. You are trusting, and believe the best of people. However, you are quite gullible and easily fooled.
COMPATIBLE LOVE PARTNER - 987
COMPATIBLE BUSINESS PARTNER - 219

KNOWN NAME NUMBER
5 Your invariable knowledge of your own importance and strength of character can lead you to be a little smug and overly confident at times, and this can offend some people.
COMPATIBLE LOVE PARTNER - 988
COMPATIBLE BUSINESS PARTNER - 211

KNOWN NAME NUMBER
6 You have a sharp tongue and aren't afraid to speak your mind—tact is not a quality you have in any abundance. You can be a little stubborn when you want to be, and may need to lighten up a bit.
COMPATIBLE LOVE PARTNER - 989
COMPATIBLE BUSINESS PARTNER - 212

Romantic gifts are the way to your heart, Known Name Number 9.

KNOWN NAME NUMBER
7 You like to socialize with friends, start new projects, and exercise your considerable power in the business world. You prefer not to be alone, and seek out the company of other people. You do not like finishing things, and hate being underemployed.
COMPATIBLE LOVE PARTNER - 981
COMPATIBLE BUSINESS PARTNER - 213

KNOWN NAME NUMBER
8 Being in love is natural for you, and you never feel quite right without a steady partner. You are also an outrageous flirt, and this can cause problems if your current lover isn't aware of how unconscious your flirtatious behavior is.
COMPATIBLE LOVE PARTNER - 982
COMPATIBLE BUSINESS PARTNER - 214

KNOWN NAME NUMBER
9 You are a great romantic, and you expect your partners to know this without telling them just how much romance you expect from them. As a result, your expectations in relationships are never quite realized.
COMPATIBLE LOVE PARTNER - 983
COMPATIBLE BUSINESS PARTNER - 215

You are a perfectionist extraordinaire, and value beauty above almost anything else. Because both your Birth Number and Full Name Number are 6, this aspect of your personality is quite strong, and is recognized by all who know you. You are also kind and loving, which saves you from being perceived as shallow. But there is still more to you waiting to be discovered. Check your Known Name Number below to find out about your hidden dimensions.

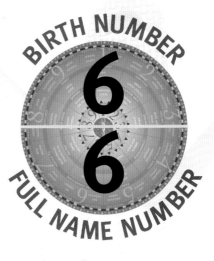

BIRTH NUMBER
6
6
FULL NAME NUMBER

KNOWN NAME NUMBER

1 You have a great passion for music and dancing, and enjoy going out, socializing, partying, and generally staying up late and indulging to excess. You are one of life's great raconteurs and love company.

COMPATIBLE LOVE PARTNER - 994
COMPATIBLE BUSINESS PARTNER - 226

KNOWN NAME NUMBER

2 Books and literature are beloved by you, and you spend long hours reading or studying. Vacations can be exhausting for you—you try to cram so much into short periods of time, and they must have a serious element.

COMPATIBLE LOVE PARTNER - 995
COMPATIBLE BUSINESS PARTNER - 227

You like to have a good time, and are by all accounts the life of the party, Known Name Number 1.

KNOWN NAME NUMBER

3 When you feel nurtured, loved, and cared for, your health is extremely strong and robust. If, however, you feel neglected or unloved, your nerves can become ragged and you may feel worn out and run down.

COMPATIBLE LOVE PARTNER - 996
COMPATIBLE BUSINESS PARTNER - 228

KNOWN NAME NUMBER

4 You have very strict rules in your life and could be seen as fussy or critical; but, in reality, you are just setting standards for others to follow. You work hard and delight in constant activity.

COMPATIBLE LOVE PARTNER - 997
COMPATIBLE BUSINESS PARTNER - 229

KNOWN NAME NUMBER

5 Although you have an excellent fashion sense and are good with fabrics, your style is a bit severe and conservative, and might even be seen as a little old-fashioned at times.

COMPATIBLE LOVE PARTNER - 998
COMPATIBLE BUSINESS PARTNER - 221

KNOWN NAME NUMBER

6 You love to acquire knowledge and don't like having your experience questioned. You research carefully before making judgments and are usually right about most things.

COMPATIBLE LOVE PARTNER - 999
COMPATIBLE BUSINESS PARTNER - 222

KNOWN NAME NUMBER

7 You have no time for lazy, indolent, or work-shy people. You are extremely physically responsive, but may be seen as emotionally detached or reserved. You are very witty and have a sophisticated, quick sense of humor.

COMPATIBLE LOVE PARTNER - 991
COMPATIBLE BUSINESS PARTNER - 223

KNOWN NAME NUMBER

8 You are extremely physically responsive, but may be seen as slightly cold. You love a good joke, and are a great storyteller. You can be quite cruel in your criticisms, as you go straight to the point and don't mask your feelings.

COMPATIBLE LOVE PARTNER - 992
COMPATIBLE BUSINESS PARTNER - 224

KNOWN NAME NUMBER

9 You fall in love with quiet dignity and are really searching for companionship. You look for partners to whom you can be devoted and for whom you have great respect. You believe in duty and responsibility towards your partners.

COMPATIBLE LOVE PARTNER - 993
COMPATIBLE BUSINESS PARTNER - 225

BIRTH NUMBER 6
FULL NAME NUMBER 7

As a Birth Number 6, you feel like you are constantly making sacrifices for everyone else and getting nothing in return. Perhaps you should lose the martyr complex and start standing up for yourself. Although you may not realize it, people do look up to you—we know this from your Full Name Number of 7. Perhaps there are other parts of yourself with which you need to get acquainted. Check your Known Name Number to find out what these may be.

KNOWN NAME NUMBER 1

You are not one of life's great romantics and may actually shy away from any overt display of romance. You like to keep your personal feelings to yourself and believe that others should do likewise.

COMPATIBLE LOVE PARTNER - 914
COMPATIBLE BUSINESS PARTNER - 236

KNOWN NAME NUMBER 2

You fear criticism and will become withdrawn if you feel insecure. You like to experiment and try new things, and are more adventurous than anyone would ever believe of you. You are also a voracious reader.

COMPATIBLE LOVE PARTNER - 915
COMPATIBLE BUSINESS PARTNER - 237

KNOWN NAME NUMBER 3

Because of your ability to pay attention to detail, you have the sort of brain that can process information; a job that utilizes this talent would be best for you—information technology or scientific research, for example.

COMPATIBLE LOVE PARTNER - 916
COMPATIBLE BUSINESS PARTNER - 238

KNOWN NAME NUMBER 4

You need your friends to hold the same sort of views as you, and you don't really like wacky or unconventional types. You like your friends to be refined, educated, tasteful, discreet, and not too emotional.

COMPATIBLE LOVE PARTNER - 917
COMPATIBLE BUSINESS PARTNER - 239

KNOWN NAME NUMBER 5

You like an easygoing life, and are very idealistic and romantic. You may be seen as frivolous because you back away from unpleasantness; but you are refined and elegant, and don't need confusion around you.

COMPATIBLE LOVE PARTNER - 918
COMPATIBLE BUSINESS PARTNER - 231

KNOWN NAME NUMBER 6

You are fairly decisive most of the time; you consider the facts carefully and then make a decision. It's true you may change your mind seconds later; but as soon as you know what it is that you want, you're totally convinced.

COMPATIBLE LOVE PARTNER - 919
COMPATIBLE BUSINESS PARTNER - 232

KNOWN NAME NUMBER 7

You are co-operative and helpful, and will go out of your way to assist friends in need. You have a formidable intellect, and would make a good teacher because you genuinely care about passing on information to others.

COMPATIBLE LOVE PARTNER - 911
COMPATIBLE BUSINESS PARTNER - 233

KNOWN NAME NUMBER 8

You have strong beliefs and are able to communicate them well. You are also extremely warm and loving, artistic, and have great taste. You would make a good diplomat because you can see both points of view.

COMPATIBLE LOVE PARTNER - 912
COMPATIBLE BUSINESS PARTNER - 234

KNOWN NAME NUMBER 9

Loud noises and loud people annoy you. You detest arguments, unless they're of the intellectual variety, in which case you can't get enough. You like going to the theater, but you don't like dressing up.

COMPATIBLE LOVE PARTNER - 913
COMPATIBLE BUSINESS PARTNER - 235

Your talent at processing information would be put to great use in the field of science, Known Name Number 3.

You are an inherently good person, Birth Number 6. You love helping others, and have a gentle nature. You believe it is your duty to care for those in need, but perhaps you shouldn't put such stress on yourself. Maybe it's because others perceive you as such a capable leader, as we know from your Full Name Number of 8, that you always end up leading the troops. Perhaps your Known Name Number below can teach you more about yourself.

BIRTH NUMBER
6
8
FULL NAME NUMBER

KNOWN NAME NUMBER

1 You enjoy being admired for your strength of character and wackiness, although a lot of it is done for effect—and you know it. You simply hate being hurried, and being told that you have to change in any way.

COMPATIBLE LOVE PARTNER - 924
COMPATIBLE BUSINESS PARTNER - 246

KNOWN NAME NUMBER

2 In public life, you may appear casual, but you are actually a stickler for tradition and historical precedent. This laissez-faire attitude of yours is all contrived; you are actually quite a traditionalist.

COMPATIBLE LOVE PARTNER - 925
COMPATIBLE BUSINESS PARTNER - 247

KNOWN NAME NUMBER

3 You are honest and industrious on the job, even if you do take ages to do anything. You are a great communicator, and that's what you do best: chatting, as others call it. You have a reputation at work as a slacker.

COMPATIBLE LOVE PARTNER - 926
COMPATIBLE BUSINESS PARTNER - 248

KNOWN NAME NUMBER

4 You are immensely friendly at work and very popular, although you probably don't think you are. You are a great one for trade unions and know your rights. You hate injustice, and always side with anyone being picked on.

COMPATIBLE LOVE PARTNER - 927
COMPATIBLE BUSINESS PARTNER - 249

Stop spending so much time talking to your friends on the telephone and start doing your job, Known Name Number 3. You are losing credibility.

KNOWN NAME NUMBER

5 The ideal occupations for you involve three key ingredients: communication, beauty, and the ability to make business deals. Get these three factors right and you will be happy in your job.

COMPATIBLE LOVE PARTNER - 928
COMPATIBLE BUSINESS PARTNER - 241

KNOWN NAME NUMBER

6 You don't like loud, uncouth people, and you expect your friends to be well groomed, sophisticated, and well read. You love discussing books, music, and the theater, and are happy to do so late into the night.

COMPATIBLE LOVE PARTNER - 929
COMPATIBLE BUSINESS PARTNER - 242

KNOWN NAME NUMBER

7 You are quite a social creature, and can get depressed if you spend too much time on your own. You recover quickly from physical illness and are not prone to emotional problems. You need more fresh air.

COMPATIBLE LOVE PARTNER - 921
COMPATIBLE BUSINESS PARTNER - 243

KNOWN NAME NUMBER

8 You are in control of yourself and are quite determined. You know what you want, how to get it, and what to do once you've got it. You suffer little or no inner turmoil, and can't stand those around you who do.

COMPATIBLE LOVE PARTNER - 922
COMPATIBLE BUSINESS PARTNER - 244

KNOWN NAME NUMBER

9 You don't have any weaknesses—or at least none that you can see. You believe in strength and purpose, and can't abide laziness, secrets being hidden from you, or being ignored. You like to be busy.

COMPATIBLE LOVE PARTNER - 923
COMPATIBLE BUSINESS PARTNER -245

BIRTH NUMBER

6

9

FULL NAME NUMBER

You are used to getting all sorts of amorous attention, attractive person that you are, Birth Number 6. Just be careful not to let it go to your head. Others see you as more than just a pretty face, however – they see you as imaginative, sensitive, and intuitive, all of which you are. But there is still more to be found behind that marvelous exterior; your Known Name Number below can help you uncover what else it is about you that is so attractive.

KNOWN NAME NUMBER

1 You don't like trusting people, especially strangers, yet you expect to be trusted yourself. But you know that isn't always the case. You think that the means justifies the end, and may be thought devious or underhanded because of this.

COMPATIBLE LOVE PARTNER - 934

COMPATIBLE BUSINESS PARTNER - 256

KNOWN NAME NUMBER

2 You feel love very intensely and can become quite dependent on your loved ones— not that they'd ever be allowed to know it. You don't like showing your emotions and positively hate any public display of affection. You can seem remote in relationships.

COMPATIBLE LOVE PARTNER - 935

COMPATIBLE BUSINESS PARTNER - 257

You rely on astrological readings to guide you, Known Name Number 7.

KNOWN NAME NUMBER

3 You like to be in charge in a relationship, and could even be called dominant. You're not particularly romantic, but can be quite tender when you want to be. You come across as being embarrassed to be in love.

COMPATIBLE LOVE PARTNER - 936

COMPATIBLE BUSINESS PARTNER - 258

KNOWN NAME NUMBER

4 You work hard and expect others to do so as well, and you can appear ruthless in your need to get a job done. You are good at solving problems and will work at something until it is right. You don't expect to fail, and rarely do.

COMPATIBLE LOVE PARTNER - 937

COMPATIBLE BUSINESS PARTNER - 259

KNOWN NAME NUMBER

5 You can process information effortlessly and make quantum leaps that others can only guess at. Because of this shrewd ability, you can see into the very depths of the souls of others, and can figure out their motives and rationales quite easily.

COMPATIBLE LOVE PARTNER - 938

COMPATIBLE BUSINESS PARTNER - 251

KNOWN NAME NUMBER

6 You are very good to your friends and always lend them a shoulder to cry on. They think you are kind, but all you really want to know is their secrets. You are a very generous person, and your home is always open to your friends and family.

COMPATIBLE LOVE PARTNER - 939

COMPATIBLE BUSINESS PARTNER - 252

KNOWN NAME NUMBER

7 Your interests invariably concern discovery. You like detective stories, research, and mysteries. You probably have a large library of books on the occult and esoteric subjects, and know a great deal about astrology.

COMPATIBLE LOVE PARTNER - 931

COMPATIBLE BUSINESS PARTNER - 253

KNOWN NAME NUMBER

8 You are a wise person, and have sound judgment and a responsible outlook on things. You value your freedom highly, and don't like discipline, rules, or routine. You seek truth and knowledge above all things.

COMPATIBLE LOVE PARTNER - 932

COMPATIBLE BUSINESS PARTNER - 254

KNOWN NAME NUMBER

9 You don't like making promises—you know you'll break them—and you simply hate being disapproved of. You are an honest person, and you resent being accused of dishonesty; you take this as a personal affront.

COMPATIBLE LOVE PARTNER - 933

COMPATIBLE BUSINESS PARTNER - 255

With a Birth Number of 7, you can be extremely intuitive—even psychic. You are also a sensitive, spiritual soul, and are prone to philosophical thoughts. Others see you as confident and capable, as is evident from your Full Name Number of 1, as well as straightforward and bright. Your Known Name Number may tell a completely different story, though; check yours below to find out about your true identity.

KNOWN NAME NUMBER

1 You have drive and a relentless ambition that propels you to the top without anyone ever realizing you were aiming there. You are charming and friendly, with a cheerful optimism that is usually lacking in such a high flier.

COMPATIBLE LOVE PARTNER - 144
COMPATIBLE BUSINESS PARTNER - 366

KNOWN NAME NUMBER

2 If more people had your approach and were less demanding, this world would be a more pleasant place. You are accommodating and helpful, always ready to lend a hand to anyone also on their way up.

COMPATIBLE LOVE PARTNER - 145
COMPATIBLE BUSINESS PARTNER - 367

KNOWN NAME NUMBER

3 You are loyal to your ideals and to your partners. When you fall in love, you will stay there for the rest of your life. There is nothing underhanded about you. You are a thoroughly nice person.

COMPATIBLE LOVE PARTNER - 146
COMPATIBLE BUSINESS PARTNER - 368

KNOWN NAME NUMBER

4 You can be outspoken and don't pull any punches when you have to speak your mind. You don't like being crossed, rejected, ignored, given the run around, or criticized.

COMPATIBLE LOVE PARTNER - 147
COMPATIBLE BUSINESS PARTNER - 369

KNOWN NAME NUMBER

5 You like honesty, activity, and travel (including mental journeys). You are also an idealistic, optimistic, cheerful soul who likes to generate new ideas and to be constantly busy.

COMPATIBLE LOVE PARTNER - 148
COMPATIBLE BUSINESS PARTNER - 361

KNOWN NAME NUMBER

6 You set your sights very high, not only for yourself but for the whole of humanity, with whom you feel an intense personal affinity. You are a visionary and a poet, an artist and a dreamer.

COMPATIBLE LOVE PARTNER - 149
COMPATIBLE BUSINESS PARTNER - 362

Some people accuse you of having your head in the clouds, Birth Number 7, but you know that you can come down to earth anytime you want to. The question is, do you want to?

KNOWN NAME NUMBER

7 You are a philosopher and an intellectual. You love to dream, have visions and goals, and yearn constantly to make this world a better place. You are driven by ambitions and internal passions that are grand in their conception and universal in their embrace.

COMPATIBLE LOVE PARTNER - 141
COMPATIBLE BUSINESS PARTNER - 363

KNOWN NAME NUMBER

8 You sincerely believe that you will be successful—if not today, then tomorrow. You remain cheerful no matter what life throws your way, and can pick yourself up from adversity quickly, springing back without any recriminations or regrets.

COMPATIBLE LOVE PARTNER - 142
COMPATIBLE BUSINESS PARTNER - 364

KNOWN NAME NUMBER

9 You are so easygoing that you are too gullible, too easy to lead astray. You can also be untidy and disorganized, and are not very punctual. You are not very good with money, and you usually forget anniversaries and promises.

COMPATIBLE LOVE PARTNER - 143
COMPATIBLE BUSINESS PARTNER - 365

BIRTH NUMBER

7

2

FULL NAME NUMBER

Travel is very important to those with a Birth Number of 7. The only time they feel truly alive is when they are on some sort of journey—be it to the nearby countryside, or to a place far away. For those who fit this bill, your Full Name Number of 2 tells us that there are people who view your tendency to just disappear from life as evidence that you hide from your responsibilities. Check your Known Name Number below to discover another side of the real you.

KNOWN NAME NUMBER

1 Some people like a challenge, but you like to wrestle life to the ground, beat it up, and then spit it out. You like to control your own destiny and to be in charge, and can be difficult when you don't get your way.

COMPATIBLE LOVE PARTNER - 154
COMPATIBLE BUSINESS PARTNER - 376

KNOWN NAME NUMBER

2 You are very impulsive and can be reckless, which sometimes necessitates you backing out of a hole you have dug for yourself. You know the old adage: when you know you're in a hole, stop digging.

COMPATIBLE LOVE PARTNER - 155
COMPATIBLE BUSINESS PARTNER - 377

KNOWN NAME NUMBER

3 You are optimistic, daring, outspoken, and cheerful. By your actions, you inspire us and make us want to be as bright, loud, and exuberant as you. You sometimes push it, though, and can be a bit overbearing.

COMPATIBLE LOVE PARTNER - 156
COMPATIBLE BUSINESS PARTNER - 378

KNOWN NAME NUMBER

5 You can be a bit of a rake, but are often forgiven because you are so charming, so refined, and so in control that people trust you and look up to you. If you are doing it, they think it can't be wrong.

COMPATIBLE LOVE PARTNER - 158
COMPATIBLE BUSINESS PARTNER - 371

You are a brave leader and a true innovator, Known Name Number 6. We need more people like you in this world.

KNOWN NAME NUMBER

4 You can be impatient in general and are often slipshod at work, but your charm and delightful personality always gets you out of trouble. You tend to be reckless, and you have a devil-may-care attitude.

COMPATIBLE LOVE PARTNER - 157
COMPATIBLE BUSINESS PARTNER - 379

KNOWN NAME NUMBER

6 If anyone is going to discover the missing link, it will be you. If anyone is prepared to start a new religion, it will be you. If anyone is going to invent a new rocket fuel, it will be you. You are always on the cutting edge.

COMPATIBLE LOVE PARTNER - 159
COMPATIBLE BUSINESS PARTNER - 372

KNOWN NAME NUMBER

7 You can be quick-tempered and impulsive. You are also impatient—you want everything and you want it now. However, you are also enthusiastic, generous, kind-hearted, and quick-thinking in emergencies.

COMPATIBLE LOVE PARTNER - 151
COMPATIBLE BUSINESS PARTNER - 373

KNOWN NAME NUMBER

8 You like to be in charge, in control, and setting the agenda. You are relentlessly energetic and optimistic, and are such a force to be reckoned with that others may see you as domineering and opinionated.

COMPATIBLE LOVE PARTNER - 152
COMPATIBLE BUSINESS PARTNER - 374

KNOWN NAME NUMBER

9 You have such enthusiasm for life that nothing holds you back for long. Any setbacks you encounter you see as challenges, not problems, and you have the ability to recover quickly from disasters.

COMPATIBLE LOVE PARTNER - 153
COMPATIBLE BUSINESS PARTNER - 375

You have a very deep inner life that you manage to keep hidden from pretty well everyone. Nobody knows the real you—how can they, when you won't let anyone in, Birth Number 7? Energetic, disciplined, and organized on the outside—a typical Full Name Number 3—you never let on that all sorts of turmoil is buzzing around inside of you. What other mysteries are you hiding? Your Known Name Number reading below tells us.

BIRTH NUMBER 7
FULL NAME NUMBER 3

KNOWN NAME NUMBER

1 You are spiritual, energetic, and strong. Because you fight our causes for us, we will follow you wherever you go. You are our savior, our leader, our hero. We look up to you.

COMPATIBLE LOVE PARTNER - 164
COMPATIBLE BUSINESS PARTNER - 386

KNOWN NAME NUMBER

2 You are open and honest in your dealings with others and expect them to be the same with you. These expectations can sometimes lead to hurt and disappointment.

COMPATIBLE LOVE PARTNER - 165
COMPATIBLE BUSINESS PARTNER - 387

KNOWN NAME NUMBER

3 You like to take risks and seem to lead a charmed life. You are relentless in your pursuit of your aspirations and will continue trying long after others have given up. This is why you are so successful.

COMPATIBLE LOVE PARTNER - 166
COMPATIBLE BUSINESS PARTNER - 388

You are a connoisseur of food and wine, Known Name Number 5, and love to throw dinner parties for your friends.

KNOWN NAME NUMBER

4 You like to be adored and in love. You enjoy being seduced and taken care of, and feel unhappy without a love interest in your life. You quickly get bored, though, and must have new interests, pursuits, and projects on the go constantly.

COMPATIBLE LOVE PARTNER - 167
COMPATIBLE BUSINESS PARTNER - 389

KNOWN NAME NUMBER

5 You hate to be kept waiting for anything. You adore gourmet food and good wines, enjoy travel and adventure, and hate boredom and routine. You would like to have lots of money, but only for the things it can buy— not for the prestige.

COMPATIBLE LOVE PARTNER - 168
COMPATIBLE BUSINESS PARTNER - 381

KNOWN NAME NUMBER

6 You are a starter, an initiator of new ideas and new projects. You will do well in any occupation where this inventive spirit is allowed to flourish. On the flip side, you will not be successful in any field in which you feel stifled and bored.

COMPATIBLE LOVE PARTNER - 169
COMPATIBLE BUSINESS PARTNER - 382

KNOWN NAME NUMBER

7 You are very creative, with strong ideas that cry out for expression. You simply hate rules, discipline, and petty tyrants. You will thrive if given the opportunity to run your own creative business.

COMPATIBLE LOVE PARTNER - 161
COMPATIBLE BUSINESS PARTNER - 383

KNOWN NAME NUMBER

8 You are not a great one for relaxing; you prefer to be working on a project, so you have something to do. When left unattended you get bored—and into trouble. And boy, can you get into trouble.

COMPATIBLE LOVE PARTNER - 162
COMPATIBLE BUSINESS PARTNER - 384

KNOWN NAME NUMBER

9 You like parties and enjoy being the life and soul of them. You enjoy themed occasions, especially when you can get dressed up and act showy and outrageous. You are quite the fun-loving dilettante.

COMPATIBLE LOVE PARTNER - 163
COMPATIBLE BUSINESS PARTNER - 385

BIRTH NUMBER 7

FULL NAME NUMBER 4

As a Birth Number 7, you are the sage that everyone else comes to for help and advice. Others have complete faith in you, and you are good at this role. Perhaps they look up to you so because they see you as practical and reliable—at least that's what your Full Name Number 4 tells us. But there are other sides to you that are just as fascinating. Your inner personality is revealed below in your Known Name Number reading.

Your sexual prowess is renowned, Known Name Number 4.

KNOWN NAME NUMBER 1

What a little charmer you are. You love socializing and being in the thick of things. You are the type of person who likes to use friends and social contacts for business deals and money-making ventures.

COMPATIBLE LOVE PARTNER - 174

COMPATIBLE BUSINESS PARTNER - 396

KNOWN NAME NUMBER 2

You are quick, lively, and very much on the ball. You love looking for opportunities, especially to increase your wealth. You have immense self-control and do not like to admit that you have emotions.

COMPATIBLE LOVE PARTNER - 175

COMPATIBLE BUSINESS PARTNER - 397

KNOWN NAME NUMBER 3

For you, family is probably more important than anything else. You are a great provider, and regard it as your duty to make sure your family wants for nothing. Indeed, providing for them is your motivating force in life.

COMPATIBLE LOVE PARTNER - 176

COMPATIBLE BUSINESS PARTNER - 398

KNOWN NAME NUMBER 4

You have tremendous sex appeal, and it is through sex that you find your true identity. With you there is no game playing or nonsense—just good old-fashioned sex that is healthy for both body and mind.

COMPATIBLE LOVE PARTNER - 177

COMPATIBLE BUSINESS PARTNER - 399

KNOWN NAME NUMBER 5

You need a partner who is as quick and lively as you, or you're inclined to get bored. If you were to find that your partner doesn't stimulate you sufficiently, you would have no qualms about taking a new lover.

COMPATIBLE LOVE PARTNER - 178

COMPATIBLE BUSINESS PARTNER - 391

KNOWN NAME NUMBER 6

You have the unique ability to be able to see which parts of an issue are important and which are irrelevant. Whatever you do, make sure you that you put this talent to good use. If you do so, you will go far.

COMPATIBLE LOVE PARTNER - 179

COMPATIBLE BUSINESS PARTNER - 392

KNOWN NAME NUMBER 7

You have quite a reputation for being good at making money. You can separate the nonsense from the imperative—and thus quickly seize the day. You are an innovator, and are always ready to rise to a challenge.

COMPATIBLE LOVE PARTNER - 171

COMPATIBLE BUSINESS PARTNER - 393

KNOWN NAME NUMBER 8

Although you may be known for your daring, you very rarely take risks, preferring instead to have worked out the odds well in advance. The only chance you take will already have been proven possible, or else you simply walk away.

COMPATIBLE LOVE PARTNER - 172

COMPATIBLE BUSINESS PARTNER - 394

KNOWN NAME NUMBER 9

You make a better boss than an underling, although you get bogged down in routine easily. You are better at igniting projects than at seeing them through, and would be best off working for yourself and having a staff execute your orders.

COMPATIBLE LOVE PARTNER - 173

COMPATIBLE BUSINESS PARTNER - 395

Just accept the fact that everyone values your opinion. People are never going to stop coming to you for advice, Birth Number 7, so stop resenting the intrusions into your time. And it's not just your advice that people seek—it's also your charming company, as your Full Name Number of 5 tells us. So lighten up and be flattered that so many think you so wise. Check your Known Name Number below for more insight into your inner personality.

BIRTH NUMBER 7

FULL NAME NUMBER 5

KNOWN NAME NUMBER

1 You are at your best in any occupation or career that allows you to develop yourself and your abilities, such as directing, administrating, or managing. You are very lively and imaginative, and are full of good ideas.

COMPATIBLE LOVE PARTNER - 184
COMPATIBLE BUSINESS PARTNER - 316

KNOWN NAME NUMBER

2 You have a knack for putting people at ease with your cheerful, outgoing, warm, and entertaining personality. You do have a tendency to talk too much, though, particularly when the subject is yourself.

COMPATIBLE LOVE PARTNER - 185
COMPATIBLE BUSINESS PARTNER - 317

KNOWN NAME NUMBER

3 You are known for your loyalty, and will stick by your friends no matter what. You are also very nonjudgmental, which certainly helps friendships along. You are very kind, which is why people like you so much.

COMPATIBLE LOVE PARTNER - 186
COMPATIBLE BUSINESS PARTNER - 318

Any job that allows you to work outdoors will make you happy, Known Name Number 8. A nine-to-five office job is definitely not for you.

KNOWN NAME NUMBER

4 You are a determined, formidable character. You are well set in your ways and have very definite opinions, all of which may seem a little old-fashioned to those who know you. You are tenacious and like to work hard.

COMPATIBLE LOVE PARTNER - 187
COMPATIBLE BUSINESS PARTNER - 319

KNOWN NAME NUMBER

5 People know they can rely on you for just about anything. You get the job done, and are a practical and sensible person. You have been known to hop off the tracks occasionally—but then who of us hasn't?

COMPATIBLE LOVE PARTNER - 188
COMPATIBLE BUSINESS PARTNER - 311

KNOWN NAME NUMBER

6 You like everyone around you, especially your family, to adhere to the same values of morality, tradition, and discipline as you do. When they fail to do so, you find it hard to cope with the rebellion.

COMPATIBLE LOVE PARTNER - 189
COMPATIBLE BUSINESS PARTNER - 312

KNOWN NAME NUMBER

7 You see everything at face value, and believe that everyone else is as honest and trustworthy as you are. Well, we're not. Or at least most of us aren't. Is that a shock? Sorry, but it's a cold, hard world out there.

COMPATIBLE LOVE PARTNER - 181
COMPATIBLE BUSINESS PARTNER - 313

KNOWN NAME NUMBER

8 In any job, you bring the same methodical, relentless spirit you do to everything in life. You are determined and strong, and don't mind a bit of fresh air or rain. This makes you ideally suited to working outdoors.

COMPATIBLE LOVE PARTNER - 182
COMPATIBLE BUSINESS PARTNER - 314

KNOWN NAME NUMBER

9 You don't like to take breaks, to be seen as lazy, or to be seen enjoying life too much. Whatever you do for a living, your goal is to work for a decent company—one that will provide security and a good pension plan.

COMPATIBLE LOVE PARTNER - 183
COMPATIBLE BUSINESS PARTNER - 315

BIRTH NUMBER
7
6
FULL NAME NUMBER

Do you ever feel like you have an inexplicable understanding of situations that you should really know nothing about? Do you often know what's going to happen before it happens? If so, this is no surprise; people with a Birth Number of 7 can be extremely psychic. Others see you as a sensual being, which, of course, you are as well. You keep the real you hidden, though. You may find that your Known Name Number below gives away some of your secret.

KNOWN NAME NUMBER

1 You don't like making promises—you know you'll break them, and you simply hate being disapproved of. You are an honest person, and resent being accused of dishonesty. You can hold a grudge for a long time.

COMPATIBLE LOVE PARTNER - 194
COMPATIBLE BUSINESS PARTNER - 326

KNOWN NAME NUMBER

2 You are honest and loyal, and you work extremely hard. Ideally, you will have a career in one of the caring professions because your cheerful disposition will enable you to get through a hard day.

COMPATIBLE LOVE PARTNER - 195
COMPATIBLE BUSINESS PARTNER - 327

KNOWN NAME NUMBER

3 You can be a little outspoken and need to be a bit more mindful of what you say. If you're not careful, that loose tongue of yours will get you into trouble. You always spring to the defense of the underdog.

COMPATIBLE LOVE PARTNER - 196
COMPATIBLE BUSINESS PARTNER - 328

KNOWN NAME NUMBER

4 You are reliable, dependable, and don't panic in a crisis. You like to speak when you have something to say, but can be quite silent the rest of the time. You think deeply about things and don't rush to conclusions.

COMPATIBLE LOVE PARTNER - 197
COMPATIBLE BUSINESS PARTNER - 329

You believe in peace and harmony, and wish that everyone would share your views, Known Name Number 6. Liberal to the core, you stand up for your convictions.

KNOWN NAME NUMBER

5 You don't like it when fun is made at your expense. Perhaps you should lighten up. You are slow to anger; but when you do blow, you do it in style. You can be prone to clumsiness if you try to move quicker than you need to.

COMPATIBLE LOVE PARTNER - 198
COMPATIBLE BUSINESS PARTNER - 321

KNOWN NAME NUMBER

6 You don't like to feel too safe or secure and enjoy challenge, adventure, and risk. You are not a great one for paperwork, rules, discipline, or authority. You are a free spirit, and march to the beat of your own drum.

COMPATIBLE LOVE PARTNER - 199
COMPATIBLE BUSINESS PARTNER - 322

KNOWN NAME NUMBER

7 Because you can read people well, the partners that you choose are usually right for you. If you do make a mistake, you will never admit that you were wrong; rather, you will endure the relationship until it ends naturally.

COMPATIBLE LOVE PARTNER - 191
COMPATIBLE BUSINESS PARTNER - 323

KNOWN NAME NUMBER

8 You enjoy the company of people who have, like you, good taste, and who appreciate the finer things in life. You don't like your friends to be too emotional, preferring a reliable, steady companionship from them.

COMPATIBLE LOVE PARTNER - 192
COMPATIBLE BUSINESS PARTNER - 324

KNOWN NAME NUMBER

9 You don't like authority, and you are a natural leader. You like to be free to follow your whims and passions, and resent being cooped up. You don't like people knowing where you've been or what you've been doing.

COMPATIBLE LOVE PARTNER - 193
COMPATIBLE BUSINESS PARTNER - 325

Your powers of intuition give your intellect a considerable boost, Birth Number 7. Indeed, you know things even before they are taught to you! The flip side of your keen intellect is that some people find you to be a bit of a know-it-all—or so your Full Name Number of 7 tells us. You know that this characterization is unfair—you just want to share your extensive knowledge. Your Known Name Number reading below can shed more light on the subject.

BIRTH NUMBER

7

7

FULL NAME NUMBER

KNOWN NAME NUMBER

1 You love people—warts, dramas, petty arguments, and all. You are simply intrigued by them, and could spend all day watching them, charting their progress, laughing at them, and observing them in minute detail.

COMPATIBLE LOVE PARTNER - 114
COMPATIBLE BUSINESS PARTNER - 336

KNOWN NAME NUMBER

2 Whatever you want to do— do it. Whatever you set your sights on, you will achieve. You have an amazing dedication to your dreams and will work extremely hard to realize your ambitions.

COMPATIBLE LOVE PARTNER - 115
COMPATIBLE BUSINESS PARTNER - 337

KNOWN NAME NUMBER

3 You have a flair for working with people, motivating them, and functioning as part of a team, and you have a great talent for getting the best out of others. Your persistence and dedication to duty is staggering.

COMPATIBLE LOVE PARTNER - 116
COMPATIBLE BUSINESS PARTNER - 338

You are wise to put some money away for a rainy day, Known Name Number 4.

KNOWN NAME NUMBER

4 Your word is your bond, and you are prepared to make sacrifices to get the job done. You worry about money quite a bit. You will probably never be wealthy, but you do like to save and provide for the future.

COMPATIBLE LOVE PARTNER - 117
COMPATIBLE BUSINESS PARTNER - 339

KNOWN NAME NUMBER

5 Always game for a laugh, you are prepared to undertake any challenge, any silly bit of nonsense, just to be liked, to be popular, and to be the center of attention. If there is one thing you hate, it is to be ignored.

COMPATIBLE LOVE PARTNER - 118
COMPATIBLE BUSINESS PARTNER - 331

KNOWN NAME NUMBER

6 You set your standards, sights, aims, and goals far too high. No one will ever be able to achieve as much as you want and expect to. You worry and care about so much and so many that you will never sleep peacefully.

COMPATIBLE LOVE PARTNER - 119
COMPATIBLE BUSINESS PARTNER - 332

KNOWN NAME NUMBER

7 You simply love a challenge, and like nothing more than to fight successfully against overwhelming odds. Give you a difficult task and you suddenly spring to life; give you a day off and you sink into depression.

COMPATIBLE LOVE PARTNER - 111
COMPATIBLE BUSINESS PARTNER - 333

KNOWN NAME NUMBER

8 You work incredibly hard and will achieve great success very young—perhaps too young, because it will spoil you. You will always seek that initial rush of fame and fortune through- out your life.

COMPATIBLE LOVE PARTNER - 112
COMPATIBLE BUSINESS PARTNER - 334

KNOWN NAME NUMBER

9 Life will deal you some unpleasant surprises that may take the form of business failures. Will you bounce back? Of course you will. If there is one talent you have, it is the ability to reinvent yourself.

COMPATIBLE LOVE PARTNER - 113
COMPATIBLE BUSINESS PARTNER - 335

BIRTH NUMBER

7

8

FULL NAME NUMBER

Birth number 7, you are a true original: psychic and intuitive on the one hand, and powerful and influential on the other. These characteristics make you an interesting person, and don't think that others don't see this. People admire your strong character, and your courage in speaking your mind, as we know from your Full Name Number of 8. Your Known Name Number below reveals your inner personality, completing the picture of what you are really all about.

KNOWN NAME NUMBER

1 You have an instinctive understanding of what makes people tick. You are spontaneous and wacky, a little unusual and outlandish, eccentric, and possibly very spiritual.

COMPATIBLE LOVE PARTNER - 124

COMPATIBLE BUSINESS PARTNER - 346

KNOWN NAME NUMBER

2 You have more energy than the rest of us put together— you are inexhaustible and relentless. It would be best if you could find a creative job that would provide a safe outlet for your insanity.

COMPATIBLE LOVE PARTNER - 125

COMPATIBLE BUSINESS PARTNER- 347

KNOWN NAME NUMBER

3 You are simply crazy, and are great fun to be around. You are also friendly and enthusiastic about everything, and are capable of changing directions so quickly that none of us can keep up with you.

COMPATIBLE LOVE PARTNER - 126

COMPATIBLE BUSINESS PARTNER - 348

You have remarkable intuition and were born with psychic powers, Birth Number 7. Your understanding of the world around you—particularly the natural world—is innate.

KNOWN NAME NUMBER

4 You have moved beyond the normal human range, and have become a sort of mental giant who has lost all touch with reality and normality. But you will be successful, wealthy, and well respected in your field.

COMPATIBLE LOVE PARTNER - 127

COMPATIBLE BUSINESS PARTNER - 349

KNOWN NAME NUMBER

5 Talented and eccentric, you go around with your head in a book or in the clouds. You remain cheerfully oblivious to the people around you. You are very bright, and you understand things that we cannot even guess at.

COMPATIBLE LOVE PARTNER - 128

COMPATIBLE BUSINESS PARTNER - 341

KNOWN NAME NUMBER

6 You can speak very well on your chosen subject— the trouble is we haven't a clue what you are talking about, as we don't understand a single word of it. Do us a favor and try to come down to our level.

COMPATIBLE LOVE PARTNER - 129

COMPATIBLE BUSINESS PARTNER - 342

KNOWN NAME NUMBER

7 You are very clever, and you want nothing more than to be universally respected and recognized as an important thinker and mental giant. You push yourself relentlessly and don't like to take breaks, relax, or unwind.

COMPATIBLE LOVE PARTNER - 121

COMPATIBLE BUSINESS PARTNER - 343

KNOWN NAME NUMBER

8 You are an extremely independent-minded person with strong views and opinions. You are very bright, and one day you will have all the fame and recognition you so obviously deserve.

COMPATIBLE LOVE PARTNER - 122

COMPATIBLE BUSINESS PARTNER - 344

KNOWN NAME NUMBER

9 Controversial and larger than life, you are not afraid to speak your mind. You are someone with whom one would not wish to argue, as you are very certain of your facts, as well as self-confident and eloquent.

COMPATIBLE LOVE PARTNER - 123

COMPATIBLE BUSINESS PARTNER - 345

Sometimes the power you have over others frightens you, Birth Number 7. You know you are psychic, and wonder if it's fair to have such a hold over the unsuspecting minds of others. But there is no need to panic about your reputation. Others do not see you as manipulative, but rather as a creative, sensitive soul, as we know from your Full Name Number of 9. The full picture of your personality is revealed in your Known Name Number reading below.

KNOWN NAME NUMBER

1 You have a bit of a problem with people who don't work as hard as you or who you think are lazy. You are very practical, and you like nothing better than to get your hands dirty and be useful around the house.

COMPATIBLE LOVE PARTNER - 134
COMPATIBLE BUSINESS PARTNER - 356

KNOWN NAME NUMBER

2 You have the capacity for hard work, persistence, and diligence, and you put these impressive qualities to use in all of your creative endeavors. As a result, you are an excellent entertainer.

COMPATIBLE LOVE PARTNER - 135
COMPATIBLE BUSINESS PARTNER - 357

KNOWN NAME NUMBER

3 You have quite a reputation for being a perfectionist at work, and you apply yourself industriously to anything you embark upon. You are often seen as a bit of a nonconformist, but this can be an asset at work.

COMPATIBLE LOVE PARTNER - 136
COMPATIBLE BUSINESS PARTNER - 358

KNOWN NAME NUMBER

4 You have a slight problem with authority, and often clash with senior management. However, you are also very good at working from the inside to get things changed. You would make a good union official.

COMPATIBLE LOVE PARTNER - 137
COMPATIBLE BUSINESS PARTNER - 359

KNOWN NAME NUMBER

5 You have quite a vision for change, and you stay true to your dreams no matter what setbacks you encounter. You are very idealistic and can be a visionary. Try to keep your feet on the ground.

COMPATIBLE LOVE PARTNER - 138
COMPATIBLE BUSINESS PARTNER - 351

KNOWN NAME NUMBER

6 You are inventive and creative, and you like to be a bit of a trendsetter. You are always at the forefront of new ways of being and new ideas. Revolutionary fervor is something you have by the bucket load.

COMPATIBLE LOVE PARTNER - 139
COMPATIBLE BUSINESS PARTNER - 352

Nothing turns you on like a good mystery, Known Name Number 9. You fancy yourself a sleuth, and gathering evidence is your specialty.

KNOWN NAME NUMBER

7 You have energy and zeal, and you like to help society. Bless you, but do we really need that much help? I think not, but thank you for trying. You are very opinionated and like to express yourself forcefully.

COMPATIBLE LOVE PARTNER - 131
COMPATIBLE BUSINESS PARTNER - 353

KNOWN NAME NUMBER

8 If there is one thing that gives you great strength, it is your altruistic approach to life— you genuinely care about how humanity is faring. Most people have a selfish or self-interested streak, but you do not.

COMPATIBLE LOVE PARTNER - 132
COMPATIBLE BUSINESS PARTNER - 354

KNOWN NAME NUMBER

9 You love knowing how things work and often see ways to make them function better. You are cool and detached in love, and prefer research to passion and investigation to lust. You are very strange indeed.

COMPATIBLE LOVE PARTNER - 133
COMPATIBLE BUSINESS PARTNER - 355

BIRTH NUMBER 8
FULL NAME NUMBER 1

The number 8 represents willpower and individuality. If this is your Birth Number, you may well be rebellious and unconventional, but you will achieve great wealth and success. Not surprisingly, you appear extremely confident and capable to the outside world, as your Full Name Number of 1 tells us. But there are other sides to you as well—more elusive, but just as interesting. Check your Known Name Number below to uncover these mysteries.

KNOWN NAME NUMBER 1

You are a visionary and an inventor, an innovator and a revolutionary. You have original thoughts and ideas and a very creative brain that rarely, if ever, switches off. Try taking a vacation once in a while.

COMPATIBLE LOVE PARTNER - 244
COMPATIBLE BUSINESS PARTNER - 466

KNOWN NAME NUMBER 2

You are eccentric, odd, rebellious, unconventional, and ever so slightly mad. You simply cannot be pigeonholed or summed up. You are as changeable as the sky. Try to be a little more predictable.

COMPATIBLE LOVE PARTNER - 245
COMPATIBLE BUSINESS PARTNER - 467

KNOWN NAME NUMBER 3

You are creative and talented, and are inclined to be slightly wild at times—but amusingly so. You can be a bit out-spoken and may even have a reputation for being difficult. Try to work more as part of a team.

COMPATIBLE LOVE PARTNER - 246
COMPATIBLE BUSINESS PARTNER - 468

KNOWN NAME NUMBER 4

You would do anything to get noticed, anything to be popular, including behaving like a fool. You like to act up, and can be amusing and entertaining. If you are clever, you will translate this behavior into a career.

COMPATIBLE LOVE PARTNER - 247
COMPATIBLE BUSINESS PARTNER - 469

You have a fear of small, confined spaces, Known Name Number 5, and are happiest when outdoors.

KNOWN NAME NUMBER 5

You hate being hemmed in or restrained, and you often feel claustrophobic. You despise things being messy or out of place, and you have a reputation at work for being a bit of a stickler for punctuality and neatness.

COMPATIBLE LOVE PARTNER - 248
COMPATIBLE BUSINESS PARTNER - 461

KNOWN NAME NUMBER 6

You like when people rely on you and would consider it a personal failure if you ever let them down. You are very hard-working, but you consider it important to take time off to be with your family.

COMPATIBLE LOVE PARTNER - 249
COMPATIBLE BUSINESS PARTNER - 462

KNOWN NAME NUMBER 7

You are dependable and reliable. You sound almost boring, and yet you manage to inject considerable humor and friendliness into everything you do. People like having you around because of your liveliness.

COMPATIBLE LOVE PARTNER - 241
COMPATIBLE BUSINESS PARTNER - 463

KNOWN NAME NUMBER 8

You know how to work hard, but you also know how to take time out and play. You enjoy a challenge, and are good at applying yourself to tasks. You are popular, successful, friendly, and well liked.

COMPATIBLE LOVE PARTNER - 242
COMPATIBLE BUSINESS PARTNER - 464

KNOWN NAME NUMBER 9

You don't like to let people down, and you will move heaven and earth to make sure that you fulfill your obligations. You have a problem with routine and hate doing menial tasks—you cannot abide dirt.

COMPATIBLE LOVE PARTNER - 243
COMPATIBLE BUSINESS PARTNER - 465

Ever since you were a child, everyone has always noted your strength of character. Well, Birth Number 8, it's the truth, and you should be proud of it. Stop projecting insecurity, as your Full Name Number 2 shows you are doing—people will not hate you because you are too "together." A better understanding of yourself might help you come across as you really are. Your Known Name Number below can provide the necessary information.

BIRTH NUMBER 8
FULL NAME NUMBER 2

Brain-teasers are your specialty, Known Name Number 2. With your agile mind, you might just unlock the secret to one of life's great mysteries.

KNOWN NAME NUMBER 1

There is only one word to really describe your work output: prodigious. You are extremely hardworking and very professional. You can seem a bit intimidating to lesser folk, so be nice to us.

COMPATIBLE LOVE PARTNER - 254
COMPATIBLE BUSINESS PARTNER - 476

KNOWN NAME NUMBER 2

You are intrigued by logic, mathematics, and puzzles of all sorts. Your clever brain lets you think in three different directions at once. You are also very practical and can fix things, which earns you kudos at home.

COMPATIBLE LOVE PARTNER - 255
COMPATIBLE BUSINESS PARTNER - 477

KNOWN NAME NUMBER 3

You are the research scientist with the heart of gold or the politician with the interest of the people at heart. You may have to wait until you are well into your middle years before you gain the recognition you deserve.

COMPATIBLE LOVE PARTNER - 256
COMPATIBLE BUSINESS PARTNER - 478

KNOWN NAME NUMBER 4

You have quite a talent for politics, as you can think quickly on your feet, are intelligent, work well with people, know how to motivate them, and will bend the rules occasionally when you feel the need dictates.

COMPATIBLE LOVE PARTNER - 257
COMPATIBLE BUSINESS PARTNER - 479

KNOWN NAME NUMBER 5

You are an arch-conservative and a stickler for courtesy and manners. You are polite and well spoken, well educated, and well read. You are an old-fashioned gentleperson, and take pride in your traditional bearing.

COMPATIBLE LOVE PARTNER - 258
COMPATIBLE BUSINESS PARTNER - 471

KNOWN NAME NUMBER 6

You are prepared to give your all if the cause is right, and you are willing to sacrifice your personal life and relationships to achieve a goal—just so long as the goal isn't too radical, extreme, or revolutionary.

COMPATIBLE LOVE PARTNER - 259
COMPATIBLE BUSINESS PARTNER - 472

KNOWN NAME NUMBER 7

You have a talent for putting people at ease, getting them to open up, and making them talk to you, which serves you well in business. You also work well as a team member. You have atrocious taste in music.

COMPATIBLE LOVE PARTNER - 251
COMPATIBLE BUSINESS PARTNER - 473

KNOWN NAME NUMBER 8

When you first start out after you leave school or university, you may be perceived as slightly mixed up and a bit vague and clueless. If only they knew what a business magnate you are going to become.

COMPATIBLE LOVE PARTNER - 252
COMPATIBLE BUSINESS PARTNER - 474

KNOWN NAME NUMBER 9

Stop putting work in front of everything else and have some fun before you get truly stressed. You could also try being a little more giving and allow others to have their foibles, quirks, and emotions.

COMPATIBLE LOVE PARTNER - 253
COMPATIBLE BUSINESS PARTNER - 475

BIRTH NUMBER

8

3

FULL NAME NUMBER

Those of you with 8 as a Birth Number typically have great organizational skills and are well respected. People see you as energetic and disciplined—just the type of person to get the job done. Your Full Name Number 3 reveals that others see you as confident. That's why they lay so much responsibility on you. But they don't know all there is to know about you. Your Known Name Number below reveals the inner elements of your personality.

KNOWN NAME NUMBER

1 You like to roll up your sleeves and get on with the job, and you dislike being distracted by anything trivial or mundane. If someone is called upon with a sense of responsibility, it will be you.

COMPATIBLE LOVE PARTNER - 264
COMPATIBLE BUSINESS PARTNER - 486

KNOWN NAME NUMBER

2 You are careful and frugal with money, but are prepared to work extremely hard to earn whatever it is you need to achieve, whatever it is you want. You hate being idle, bored, ill, restless, distracted, or indulged.

COMPATIBLE LOVE PARTNER - 265
COMPATIBLE BUSINESS PARTNER - 487

KNOWN NAME NUMBER

3 You can be relied upon in a crisis, and depended upon when the going gets tough. You face up to your responsibilities, and always seek excellence in life—and also the means to purchase it.

COMPATIBLE LOVE PARTNER - 266
COMPATIBLE BUSINESS PARTNER - 488

KNOWN NAME NUMBER

4 You are full of stamina, and you can work or party long after the others have fallen by the wayside. You have limitless enthusiasm for the latest craze or fad, and you seem to enjoy life rather too much.

COMPATIBLE LOVE PARTNER - 267
COMPATIBLE BUSINESS PARTNER - 489

KNOWN NAME NUMBER

5 You have a bit of a reputation for being a trifle difficult to work with, as you set pretty high standards. You are blessed with enormous creative talent, but like many artists, you can be pushy and demanding.

COMPATIBLE LOVE PARTNER - 268
COMPATIBLE BUSINESS PARTNER - 481

KNOWN NAME NUMBER

6 You are fun to be around, but it is no fun to be on the receiving end of your acerbic sense of humor. You can be quite cruel, cutting, snobbish, and pompous. But you are so charming and refined that you get away with it.

COMPATIBLE LOVE PARTNER - 269
COMPATIBLE BUSINESS PARTNER - 482

Your curiosity is limitless, Known Name Number 9. You are constantly reading obscure texts, searching for the answers to your strange but intriguing questions.

KNOWN NAME NUMBER

7 If there is a solution to be found, you will find it, no matter how elusive it may be. If there are people to motivate, you will motivate them. You can be very outspoken, but only when there is a real need to get a point across.

COMPATIBLE LOVE PARTNER - 261
COMPATIBLE BUSINESS PARTNER - 483

KNOWN NAME NUMBER

8 You are kind and sympathetic, with true compassion and genuine concern for others. You aren't particularly money-orientated or ambitious; you are more concerned with finding out how the world works.

COMPATIBLE LOVE PARTNER - 262
COMPATIBLE BUSINESS PARTNER - 484

KNOWN NAME NUMBER

9 Your interests are wacky and unusual; you love the abnormal and the paranormal. You like to find out new things, and are an avid reader. You are inquisitive about the world, and will never lose your fascination with nature.

COMPATIBLE LOVE PARTNER - 263
COMPATIBLE BUSINESS PARTNER - 485

You work well in a team, Birth Number 8, especially when you are leading it. You can push a bit hard, but that is often what it takes to get the job done. Others respond well to your leadership because they see you as reliable— they know that you would do anything for your "troops." That is why they are so faithful to you, Full Name Number 4. But is this confidence in you deserved? Your Known Name Number below can help you find out.

BIRTH NUMBER 8
FULL NAME NUMBER 4

KNOWN NAME NUMBER

1 Sometimes you are just too loud or too much to take, but people are usually pleased to see you. You can be impatient and slipshod at work, but your charm and winning personality usually get you out of trouble.

COMPATIBLE LOVE PARTNER - 274
COMPATIBLE BUSINESS PARTNER - 496

KNOWN NAME NUMBER

2 By your actions, you inspire us and make us want to be as bright, loud, and exuberant as you. You are optimistic, daring, outspoken, and very cheerful. You are awe-inspiring in your bravery.

COMPATIBLE LOVE PARTNER - 275
COMPATIBLE BUSINESS PARTNER - 497

Fine art is a passion of yours, Known Name Number 4, and you are quite artistic yourself.

KNOWN NAME NUMBER

3 You spend all of your time networking, being in the thick of the action, being busy, being indispensable, being in demand, and being rich. You work hard, but could be more discerning about the jobs you take on.

COMPATIBLE LOVE PARTNER - 276
COMPATIBLE BUSINESS PARTNER - 498

KNOWN NAME NUMBER

4 You love to travel, collect fine art, and visit museums and art galleries abroad. You are a bit of an optimist in this way—free-thinking and full of new ideas and projects. You are never down for too long.

COMPATIBLE LOVE PARTNER - 277
COMPATIBLE BUSINESS PARTNER - 499

KNOWN NAME NUMBER

5 You love fun and the good things in life. You are a kind, sympathetic character who listens well to others' problems— and tries to help solve them. You like to be surrounded by people and are extremely popular.

COMPATIBLE LOVE PARTNER - 278
COMPATIBLE BUSINESS PARTNER - 491

KNOWN NAME NUMBER

6 You don't like to fail, which can drive you on—even to excess at times. You are very clever and use your mind to great advantage. You are successful, practical, and reliable, both at work and at home.

COMPATIBLE LOVE PARTNER - 279
COMPATIBLE BUSINESS PARTNER - 492

KNOWN NAME NUMBER

7 You are unceasingly busy, almost to the point of mania. You simply don't know how to relax or rest, and this can cause stress-related health problems if you aren't careful. Take a vacation at once.

COMPATIBLE LOVE PARTNER- 271
COMPATIBLE BUSINESS PARTNER - 493

KNOWN NAME NUMBER

8 You are quick, decisive, and sharp. No one pulls a fast one on you, and you love to get the better of a deal or bargain. You like nothing better than making money out of what other people discard.

COMPATIBLE LOVE PARTNER - 272
COMPATIBLE BUSINESS PARTNER - 494

KNOWN NAME NUMBER

9 You make a formidable opponent when discussing business deals, and have a reputation for being ruthless. You could try letting others see a softer, gentler side of you—you do have one, in case you'd forgotten.

COMPATIBLE LOVE PARTNER - 273
COMPATIBLE BUSINESS PARTNER - 495

BIRTH NUMBER

8
5

FULL NAME NUMBER

You often drive yourself—and others—crazy with your quest for perfection. You can't help it though; perfectionism is a common trait for Birth Number 8. Lucky for you, people see you as charming, witty, and fun to be around, as we know from your Full Name Number of 5. But this is not the whole story. There is so much more to you—perhaps more than you care to admit. Check your Known Name Number below. You may be surprised at what you find out.

KNOWN NAME NUMBER

1 You are up before anyone else and already busy with the day's work. You are out there buying and selling while others are still lingering over breakfast. And when others go home for the day, you are still wheeling and dealing.

COMPATIBLE LOVE PARTNER - 284
COMPATIBLE BUSINESS PARTNER - 416

KNOWN NAME NUMBER

2 You have a wonderful, easygoing attitude, and are very easy to get along with—even if it is all a sham. You don't particularly like to work with your hands, as you are a thinker—or rather, a schemer.

COMPATIBLE LOVE PARTNER - 285
COMPATIBLE BUSINESS PARTNER - 417

KNOWN NAME NUMBER

3 You aren't a great one for relaxing, and anything you do to wind down usually involves some element of work. You like to be busy, but this will lead to health problems if you don't learn to switch off occasionally.

COMPATIBLE LOVE PARTNER - 286
COMPATIBLE BUSINESS PARTNER - 418

When work calls, you come running, Known Name Numbers 1 and 3. Your career comes before everything else in your life—even your friends and family.

KNOWN NAME NUMBER

4 Some people think you are sleepy and slow; others think you stubborn and set in your ways. Neither of these perceptions are true, of course. The truth about you is much deeper than that, as you well know.

COMPATIBLE LOVE PARTNER - 287
COMPATIBLE BUSINESS PARTNER - 419

KNOWN NAME NUMBER

5 You are a curious anomaly in this modern world— someone who actually cares about old-fashioned values. Indeed, values are what you are all about. They may hold you back, though, so be careful.

COMPATIBLE LOVE PARTNER - 288
COMPATIBLE BUSINESS PARTNER - 411

KNOWN NAME NUMBER

6 Everything seems to move too fast, too furiously, for you these days. You prefer calm and peacefulness, order and routine. You are a sentimental romantic from a bygone age. Perhaps it's time you joined us here in the present.

COMPATIBLE LOVE PARTNER - 289
COMPATIBLE BUSINESS PARTNER - 412

KNOWN NAME NUMBER

7 You are a worrier by nature. You worry that the world has gone to the dogs and that no one does a good job any more. You also worry about what the future will bring, especially for your children.

COMPATIBLE LOVE PARTNER - 281
COMPATIBLE BUSINESS PARTNER - 413

KNOWN NAME NUMBER

8 You believe in order, ritual, and tradition, and don't take to new ideas very quickly. Quite often, you are misunderstood. You are the strong, silent type who keeps to yourself. Few people can read your thoughts.

COMPATIBLE LOVE PARTNER - 282
COMPATIBLE BUSINESS PARTNER - 414

KNOWN NAME NUMBER

9 You are a very loyal friend, and you pay attention to duty. If ever I needed a true friend to be there in a time of crisis, it would be you I would choose. But if someone crosses you, watch out. You can be quite vengeful.

COMPATIBLE LOVE PARTNER - 283
COMPATIBLE BUSINESS PARTNER - 415

If your Birth Number is 8, chances are you are not afraid to speak your mind, and you don't care if your opinion is unpopular. This often comes as a surprise to those who don't know you very well. Many of your acquaintances and colleagues see you as lighthearted, as we know from your Full Name Number of 6. They have no idea that such conviction lurks behind that carefree exterior. Your Known Name Number below reveals another side to you.

BIRTH NUMBER 8

FULL NAME NUMBER 6

You have superb organizational skills, Known Name Numbers 1 and 2, and would be fantastic at public relations or event planning.

KNOWN NAME NUMBER

1 You are excellent at organizing things—anything from a simple children's party to a pop concert for thirty thousand. You are an honest, moral person, and wouldn't know how to lie—even if you wanted to.

COMPATIBLE LOVE PARTNER - 294

COMPATIBLE BUSINESS PARTNER - 426

KNOWN NAME NUMBER

2 You are an unbelievably hardworking person who shuns the limelight and prefers to work backstage, organizing the event. Without you, the show simply couldn't go on. You just give everyone else the credit.

COMPATIBLE LOVE PARTNER - 295

COMPATIBLE BUSINESS PARTNER - 427

KNOWN NAME NUMBER

3 You are very good with people, and you are tolerant and patient. You do set high standards, though, and don't take kindly to sloth or dishonesty in the workplace. You are a stickler for obeying rules.

COMPATIBLE LOVE PARTNER - 296

COMPATIBLE BUSINESS PARTNER - 428

KNOWN NAME NUMBER

4 You don't really know how to relax, do you? You work until you drop and then complain about exhaustion. When you do take time off, you occupy your time gardening or socializing. Some rest would be good for you.

COMPATIBLE LOVE PARTNER - 297

COMPATIBLE BUSINESS PARTNER - 429

KNOWN NAME NUMBER

5 Anyone falling in love with you will get a very high return on their investment, as you give your whole heart and soul to the relationship—and your heart and soul are very big indeed. You are a true romantic.

COMPATIBLE LOVE PARTNER - 298

COMPATIBLE BUSINESS PARTNER - 421

KNOWN NAME NUMBER

6 You have great strength of body and character, and were born to lead, even if no one is following yet. You love a good fight and being in trouble. There is virtually no subject that you cannot talk about intelligently.

COMPATIBLE LOVE PARTNER - 299

COMPATIBLE BUSINESS PARTNER - 422

KNOWN NAME NUMBER

7 Life for you would be boring if you weren't always planning the next great adventure. You are one of life's motivators, and the planet would be dull without you around. You have a love of foreign religions.

COMPATIBLE LOVE PARTNER - 291

COMPATIBLE BUSINESS PARTNER - 423

KNOWN NAME NUMBER

8 You are brave and reckless on the outside—and quite rightly so, as you certainly have the qualities of daring and courage in abundance. But in your head, you often feel lonely and unloved. Start reaching out more to others.

COMPATIBLE LOVE PARTNER - 292

COMPATIBLE BUSINESS PARTNER - 424

KNOWN NAME NUMBER

9 You make rash and impulsive decisions at times, and are forced to live with the consequences. The good news is that you will mellow as you grow older and will eventually end up a calm, contented pussycat.

COMPATIBLE LOVE PARTNER - 293

COMPATIBLE BUSINESS PARTNER - 425

BIRTH NUMBER 8

FULL NAME NUMBER 7

When put in a group situation, you always wind up taking control. Well, why not? You're good at leading others, right Birth Number 8? Just beware of the image that you project to others. Although they respect you, they sometimes find you frighteningly cold, or so your Full Name Number of 7 tells us. Maybe you can find a happy medium after all. Check your Known Name Number reading below for a sense of what you're really capable of.

KNOWN NAME NUMBER

1 You have many friends who think the world of you, even if you exhaust them. You do like to be in charge, though, and should give your friends a little more say in how you socialize.
COMPATIBLE LOVE PARTNER - 214
COMPATIBLE BUSINESS PARTNER - 436

KNOWN NAME NUMBER

2 You like to take risks and fly high, so you will not be successful at any job in which you feel trapped. Be an explorer and you'll go far, although you may suffer setbacks due to your nature.
COMPATIBLE LOVE PARTNER - 215
COMPATIBLE BUSINESS PARTNER - 437

KNOWN NAME NUMBER

3 You don't really have any leisure time, as you're always so busy working on projects and doing other things. The way you relax may seem like hard work to everyone else, but you really do enjoy being creative and active.
COMPATIBLE LOVE PARTNER - 216
COMPATIBLE BUSINESS PARTNER - 438

KNOWN NAME NUMBER

4 You feel best when you are in love, and you are a great romantic. You give everything in love and feel hurt if let down. You do lose interest easily, however, and like to move on. You can be very unconventional at times.
COMPATIBLE LOVE PARTNER - 217
COMPATIBLE BUSINESS PARTNER - 439

KNOWN NAME NUMBER

5 You have enormous energy for love, and your intensity can wear out a lesser soul. You are affectionate, caring, and loving, and you simply glow when you are loved in return. You fall in love easily and often.
COMPATIBLE LOVE PARTNER - 218
COMPATIBLE BUSINESS PARTNER - 431

KNOWN NAME NUMBER

6 You have limitless energy, boundless enthusiasm, and a very fertile imagination. What more could anyone want? Perhaps a bit of gentleness and attention now and again. You are very trustworthy, and can be relied upon.
COMPATIBLE LOVE PARTNER - 219
COMPATIBLE BUSINESS PARTNER - 432

You seek justice, and are adept at getting others to confess to their crimes to you, Known Name Number 7.

KNOWN NAME NUMBER

7 You just pretend to be crazy, so that people will tell you more than they should. You're good at getting information out of people, cross-examining them until they tell you the truth. You would make a good lawyer.
COMPATIBLE LOVE PARTNER - 211
COMPATIBLE BUSINESS PARTNER - 433

KNOWN NAME NUMBER

8 You are quick and sharp-witted, and no one has ever been able to put one over on you. You are, however, unpredictable, and no one really knows how they stand with you. You can be very intense and a little difficult.
COMPATIBLE LOVE PARTNER - 212
COMPATIBLE BUSINESS PARTNER - 434

KNOWN NAME NUMBER

9 You are a loner, although one can always find you surrounded by crowds of people. You are gifted and talented, and are adept at handling tricky situations. You are capable and controlled, in charge and up front.
COMPATIBLE LOVE PARTNER - 213
COMPATIBLE BUSINESS PARTNER - 435

Ever since you were a child, you have always had a rebellious streak in you, Birth Number 8. Now that you are an adult, your chutzpah is paying off in the business world, and you are proud of yourself. Other people recognize you as a leader and innovator—as your Full Name Number 8 tells us—which is why you are so successful. But are you as perfect as you seem? Your Known Name Number reading below can help you answer this question.

BIRTH NUMBER
8
8
FULL NAME NUMBER

Keep on conducting those madcap experiments, Known Name Number 1. Who knows, one day you might discover something groundbreaking and win a Nobel Prize.

KNOWN NAME NUMBER

1 Your work is very important to you. You are so bright and clever that if you aren't employed using your brains, you are being wasted. You are a researcher, an inventor, and a mad scientist.

COMPATIBLE LOVE PARTNER - 224
COMPATIBLE BUSINESS PARTNER - 446

KNOWN NAME NUMBER

2 You have a unique way of thinking that allows you to make quantum leaps of imagination and logic that we mere mortals can only dream of. You are one of the great lateral thinkers of this world.

COMPATIBLE LOVE PARTNER - 225
COMPATIBLE BUSINESS PARTNER - 447

KNOWN NAME NUMBER

3 You have a somewhat quirky sense of humor, and people often raise their eyebrows at how coarse you can be at times. This behavior is incongruous with your other refinements and your love of quality and good taste.

COMPATIBLE LOVE PARTNER - 226
COMPATIBLE BUSINESS PARTNER - 448

KNOWN NAME NUMBER

4 You are a very private person, and your partner may complain that he or she never really knows where they stand with you. Perhaps you should open up a bit and share your feelings a little more readily.

COMPATIBLE LOVE PARTNER - 227
COMPATIBLE BUSINESS PARTNER - 449

KNOWN NAME NUMBER

5 You are larger than life, twice as grand as anybody else, twice as fabulous and ten times more superb. But I don't know why I am telling you all this—you already know it. It's in your nature.

COMPATIBLE LOVE PARTNER - 228
COMPATIBLE BUSINESS PARTNER - 441

KNOWN NAME NUMBER

6 You are one of those people that others turn to for advice, information, and opinions. People value what you have to say, and regard it as a great honor when you share your views with them.

COMPATIBLE LOVE PARTNER - 229
COMPATIBLE BUSINESS PARTNER - 442

KNOWN NAME NUMBER

7 You hate being bored, poor, or lied to—and why not, for you are important and irreplaceable. The world would be a duller place without you to inspire the rest of us. You are the guardian of our spiritual heritage.

COMPATIBLE LOVE PARTNER - 221
COMPATIBLE BUSINESS PARTNER - 443

KNOWN NAME NUMBER

8 You don't really like work, do you? Oh, you like the status, the money, the position, and the kudos—but the actual work? Not your cup of tea. Luckily for you, you don't ever have to work too hard.

COMPATIBLE LOVE PARTNER - 222
COMPATIBLE BUSINESS PARTNER - 444

KNOWN NAME NUMBER

9 You have such a natural air of authority about you that you get elevated to positions of power and importance without ever really having to do anything. You are a born leader of the boardroom.

COMPATIBLE LOVE PARTNER - 223
COMPATIBLE BUSINESS PARTNER - 445

BIRTH NUMBER
8
9
FULL NAME NUMBER

When something needs doing, you hunker down and do it. That's what's so great about you, Birth Number 8, and it's a trait that others admire. You may not know this, but people also respect your courage in always sticking up for the underdogs of this world; we know this from your Full Name Number of 9. What else do you have to offer this world? Quite a bit, I imagine. Your Known Name Number below reveals more about your inner personality.

People love being around you, Known Name Numbers 4 and 5. Perhaps it's your charming, caring demeanor.

KNOWN NAME NUMBER

1 Your character is deep and unfathomable—at least that's what most people think. But, in reality, you are very easy to understand and know. If only people wouldn't be so hasty .

COMPATIBLE LOVE PARTNER - 236

COMPATIBLE BUSINESS PARTNER - 458

KNOWN NAME NUMBER

2 You can be charming and debonair, sophisticated and elegant. You can also be ruthless and cruel, manipulative and calculating. You can be many things. Which is the real you?

COMPATIBLE LOVE PARTNER - 234

COMPATIBLE BUSINESS PARTNER - 456

KNOWN NAME NUMBER

3 For you, the means always justify the end. If a problem needs solving, you solve it. However, sometimes you may sail a little close to the wind when it comes to finding solutions.

COMPATIBLE LOVE PARTNER - 235

COMPATIBLE BUSINESS PARTNER - 457

KNOWN NAME NUMBER

4 You are romantic and sensuous, and you have a very subtle sense of humor. You love nothing better than to be surrounded by admirers and having the world wait on your next word.

COMPATIBLE LOVE PARTNER - 237

COMPATIBLE BUSINESS PARTNER - 459

KNOWN NAME NUMBER

5 You are a kind, sympathetic character who listens well to others' problems—you even do your best to help solve them. You like to be surrounded by people, and you are extremely popular and well loved.

COMPATIBLE LOVE PARTNER - 238

COMPATIBLE BUSINESS PARTNER - 451

KNOWN NAME NUMBER

6 You have a wonderful sense of humor, although it can be a little ironic and teasing at times. You are very loving and caring. You are good and quick with your hands, and you are creative and practical.

COMPATIBLE LOVE PARTNER - 239

COMPATIBLE BUSINESS PARTNER - 452

KNOWN NAME NUMBER

7 You are a born gossip, although you certainly are a good friend. Some of your friends would be touched to realize how much you care about them, although you rarely let your true feelings show.

COMPATIBLE LOVE PARTNER - 231

COMPATIBLE BUSINESS PARTNER - 453

KNOWN NAME NUMBER

8 You are attractive and vivacious, although you feign humility about your good looks. You don't compromise in any circumstances, and you hold very strong views about how the world should be.

COMPATIBLE LOVE PARTNER - 232

COMPATIBLE BUSINESS PARTNER - 454

KNOWN NAME NUMBER

9 You set an example for us all. You are loyal and trustworthy, friendly and enterprising, cheerful and sincere. You probably don't realize what an inspiration you are to the rest of us—or maybe you do.

COMPATIBLE LOVE PARTNER - 233

COMPATIBLE BUSINESS PARTNER - 455

If your Birth Number is 9, you are probably a very expressive person. This expression can take a number of forms: painting, writing, composing music—all of these activities make you happy. Some people find you intimidating and exhausting, according to your Full Name Number of 1. But you are infinitely more complex than this. Check your Known Name Number reading below; you may want to bring your inner personality to the fore.

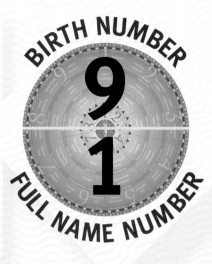

BIRTH NUMBER 9

FULL NAME NUMBER 1

KNOWN NAME NUMBER

1 You have never learned the meaning of the word "can't." You simply do. You are a true pragmatist. You aren't wacky or unconventional in your approach, which means you get the job done quickly and efficiently.

COMPATIBLE LOVE PARTNER - 344
COMPATIBLE BUSINESS PARTNER - 566

KNOWN NAME NUMBER

2 You are resourceful and versatile, and are able to turn your hand to pretty well anything you choose, just so long as you agree with the principles and morals involved. You like to stay on the right side of the law.

COMPATIBLE LOVE PARTNER - 345
COMPATIBLE BUSINESS PARTNER - 567

The rigid schedule of a nine-to-five job is not for you, Known Name Number 5. A career that involves travel and adventure would be ideal for you.

KNOWN NAME NUMBER

3 You are an independent character with a mind of your own, and you are always willing to share your opinions with others. If there's one thing you are renowned for, it's your gregarious and talkative nature.

COMPATIBLE LOVE PARTNER - 346
COMPATIBLE BUSINESS PARTNER - 568

KNOWN NAME NUMBER

4 You are a kind person who genuinely cares about those around you, but you don't care too much about world politics or the state of the nation—all that matters to you is that your loved ones are well fed and happy.

COMPATIBLE LOVE PARTNER - 347
COMPATIBLE BUSINESS PARTNER - 569

KNOWN NAME NUMBER

5 You can do anything that requires talking, thinking fast on your feet, being versatile, and being talented. You don't like routine, and are best suited to jobs in which you have the freedom to move around.

COMPATIBLE LOVE PARTNER - 348
COMPATIBLE BUSINESS PARTNER - 561

KNOWN NAME NUMBER

6 The key word for you is communication—and this is where you will find the best job for yourself. You may not be a brilliant ideas person, but you can certainly convey ideas to other people, even if the ideas are not your own.

COMPATIBLE LOVE PARTNER - 349
COMPATIBLE BUSINESS PARTNER - 562

KNOWN NAME NUMBER

7 You have a reputation for being manipulative, but that's only because you are so quick to see how a situation can benefit you. If the rest of us are too slow, then who can blame you for taking advantage of us?

COMPATIBLE LOVE PARTNER - 341
COMPATIBLE BUSINESS PARTNER - 563

KNOWN NAME NUMBER

8 You like to break the rules. This can get you into trouble sometimes, but you usually talk your way out of it. You are a risk-taker and a gambler, and have been known to lie through your teeth to get what you want.

COMPATIBLE LOVE PARTNER - 342
COMPATIBLE BUSINESS PARTNER - 564

KNOWN NAME NUMBER

9 People may accuse you of having no depth, but in reality you do think quite deeply about things. It's just that on the surface you seem so carefree. You make light of your feelings and always say that everything is fine.

COMPATIBLE LOVE PARTNER - 343
COMPATIBLE BUSINESS PARTNER - 565

BIRTH NUMBER

9

2

FULL NAME NUMBER

You are a poet at heart, Birth Number 9. Creative and imaginative, if you could spend all of your time exploring the depths of the human soul, you would. On the outside, you get along well with people, and are caring and supportive—at least according to your Full Name Number of 2. It seems like you've got it all, but I'm sure you know there is more to you than meets the eye. In your Known Name Number reading below you will find your inner personality revealed.

KNOWN NAME NUMBER

1 You are known for your honesty and quick wit. You are a capable, practical sort of person who can fix things, make things, and generally be useful. You like your independence.

COMPATIBLE LOVE PARTNER - 354
COMPATIBLE BUSINESS PARTNER - 576

KNOWN NAME NUMBER

2 You don't stay still for very long. You need a job that gives you a lot of independence and trust, because you hate having anyone breathing down your neck or looking over your shoulder.

COMPATIBLE LOVE PARTNER - 355
COMPATIBLE BUSINESS PARTNER - 577

KNOWN NAME NUMBER

3 You love being refined and well-to-do, and take great pride in your personal appearance. You want to be somebody, do something impressive. You have lofty ambitions, and you work hard to achieve them.

COMPATIBLE LOVE PARTNER - 356
COMPATIBLE BUSINESS PARTNER - 578

KNOWN NAME NUMBER

4 You are intelligent and have a fine eye for detail. You take great care about your appearance, and some might say you're a bit of a dandy. You are very popular and are appreciated by your friends.

COMPATIBLE LOVE PARTNER - 357
COMPATIBLE BUSINESS PARTNER - 579

KNOWN NAME NUMBER

5 You are ambitious, but don't particularly like taking orders; you'd better climb the ladder as quickly as possible, so you won't have to. The trouble is, you are also supremely lazy. What are you going to do?

COMPATIBLE LOVE PARTNER - 358
COMPATIBLE BUSINESS PARTNER - 571

KNOWN NAME NUMBER

6 You want your needs to be attended to immediately. You like always to be served first, and you can be a little egocentric, but you are always enthusiastic and energetic. You are very trustworthy and loving.

COMPATIBLE LOVE PARTNER - 359
COMPATIBLE BUSINESS PARTNER - 572

You are very good with your hands, Known Name Number 1, and can make or fix just about anything. If you wished to, you could start a business selling your hand-crafted items. It would no doubt be very successful.

KNOWN NAME NUMBER

7 If someone needs a friend, you are there. If someone needs a shoulder to cry on, it's probably your shoulder they choose. You're a loyal, faithful companion. The really nice thing about you is your tolerance.

COMPATIBLE LOVE PARTNER - 351
COMPATIBLE BUSINESS PARTNER - 573

KNOWN NAME NUMBER

8 You are incredibly idealistic —always trying to create a world full of love, peace, and harmony. You hate conflict and confrontation, although you can cope with them if they arise. Some people see you as self-righteous.

COMPATIBLE LOVE PARTNER - 352
COMPATIBLE BUSINESS PARTNER - 574

KNOWN NAME NUMBER

9 You have an enormous heart, and care so deeply about the state of things that you spend a lot of time in tears at the unfairness of it all. You are also ambitious, and have a gift for seeing into other people's souls.

COMPATIBLE LOVE PARTNER - 353
COMPATIBLE BUSINESS PARTNER - 575

What a great champion of the underdog you are, Birth Number 9! Congratulations. Standing up for the rights of others takes courage and conviction, both of which you have in abundance. You come off as very sure of yourself, according to your Full Name Number of 3, which helps you in your quest to convince others to join you in your crusades. Your Known Name Number reading below casts some light on your enigmatic inner persona.

BIRTH NUMBER
9
3
FULL NAME NUMBER

KNOWN NAME NUMBER

1 We know you like your independence, so what's the beef? We also know you are headstrong and outgoing, and have no wish to curb your freedom. Stop being so argumentative.

COMPATIBLE LOVE PARTNER - 364
COMPATIBLE BUSINESS PARTNER - 586

KNOWN NAME NUMBER

2 For some of us, this life is just a learning experience. For you, however, it is purely fun. This is a life off for you, and you can coast as much as you want without concern. Enjoy your freedom.

COMPATIBLE LOVE PARTNER - 365
COMPATIBLE BUSINESS PARTNER - 587

KNOWN NAME NUMBER

3 You like being busy and active—but is all this a front to stop you from thinking? You will have to face your inner demons one day; better to get it over with. You have the courage, so what is holding you back?

COMPATIBLE LOVE PARTNER - 366
COMPATIBLE BUSINESS PARTNER - 588

People are attracted to you because of your considerable charisma and magnetism, Known Name Number 9.

KNOWN NAME NUMBER

4 If you are not a politician, then what are you wasting your time on? You have a caring side that needs an outlet, and politics takes into account your considerable communication and motivational skills.

COMPATIBLE LOVE PARTNER - 367
COMPATIBLE BUSINESS PARTNER - 589

KNOWN NAME NUMBER

5 What a charmer you are. You love socializing and being in the thick of things. You have no problem with using your friends and social contacts for business deals and money-making ventures. Luckily, they trust you.

COMPATIBLE LOVE PARTNER - 368
COMPATIBLE BUSINESS PARTNER - 581

KNOWN NAME NUMBER

6 You are quick, lively, and very much on the ball. You love looking for opportunities, especially to increase your wealth. You are quite self-controlled and don't like to admit that you have emotions, let alone show them.

COMPATIBLE LOVE PARTNER - 369
COMPATIBLE BUSINESS PARTNER - 582

KNOWN NAME NUMBER

7 You certainly have a way with the opposite sex, being charming and very entertaining. You can seduce pretty well anyone you take a liking to—and, by golly, there are quite a few of those around at any time.

COMPATIBLE LOVE PARTNER - 361
COMPATIBLE BUSINESS PARTNER - 583

KNOWN NAME NUMBER

8 You have a very good memory, which serves you well when you need it. You pick up skills very quickly indeed, possess a sharp intelligence, and can make decisions with extraordinary speed and confidence.

COMPATIBLE LOVE PARTNER - 362
COMPATIBLE BUSINESS PARTNER - 584

KNOWN NAME NUMBER

9 You find it extremely easy to talk to people. They, in turn, are powerfully drawn to you due to your personality and charm. Your friends find you witty, amusing, and lots of fun to be with and to have around.

COMPATIBLE LOVE PARTNER - 363
COMPATIBLE BUSINESS PARTNER - 585

BIRTH NUMBER

9
4

FULL NAME NUMBER

Those with a Birth Number of 9 find themselves drawn to the exotic, even freakish, elements of life. They are what makes life worth living, right? Isn't it funny then that despite the strange company you keep, people would still describe you as down-to-earth—the practical, reliable type, as we know from your Full Name Number of 4. Why this dichotomy in your personality? Perhaps your Known Name Number reading below can shed some light on this question.

KNOWN NAME NUMBER

1 You love socializing and would drop anything to go partying, chatting, whatever. You just adore being around people. You love work, so long as you can network. You are a bit of a name-dropper.

COMPATIBLE LOVE PARTNER - 374
COMPATIBLE BUSINESS PARTNER - 596

KNOWN NAME NUMBER

2 Work is very important to you, and it is where your critical side can be used to great effect. You have an eye for detail and like to see a job through no matter what. You have the tendency to be a workaholic and should learn to relax a bit.

COMPATIBLE LOVE PARTNER - 375
COMPATIBLE BUSINESS PARTNER - 597

KNOWN NAME NUMBER

3 You are very good at solving problems, finding solutions, and spotting faults. You would make a good engineer. You would also make a good money manager, although you might not be effective at managing your own.

COMPATIBLE LOVE PARTNER - 376
COMPATIBLE BUSINESS PARTNER - 598

KNOWN NAME NUMBER

4 When you apply yourself at work, you succeed. Your ambitions will be fulfilled easily, just so long as you don't clash with the boss. You cannot work for any-one you think foolish, lazy, or incompetent.

COMPATIBLE LOVE PARTNER - 377
COMPATIBLE BUSINESS PARTNER - 599

KNOWN NAME NUMBER

5 If you allow anyone to get close to you, then they become friends—and very loyal friends—for life. The trouble is that the harsh façade you put up, combined with your critical nature, can put people off.

COMPATIBLE LOVE PARTNER - 378
COMPATIBLE BUSINESS PARTNER - 591

KNOWN NAME NUMBER

6 This outspoken front you put up is just that—a front. If and when you decide to drop it, you are warm and friendly, supportive and loyal, kind and generous, and a very trusty friend indeed.

COMPATIBLE LOVE PARTNER - 379
COMPATIBLE BUSINESS PARTNER - 592

You have a caring, nurturing personality, and are best suited to a career that will allow you to help others, Known Name Number 8.

KNOWN NAME NUMBER

7 You are just too easygoing to devote time and energy to work, and you prefer to socialize and shop. Some people might think you are shallow and spoiled, but you really don't care. Good for you.

COMPATIBLE LOVE PARTNER - 371
COMPATIBLE BUSINESS PARTNER - 593

KNOWN NAME NUMBER

8 If you devote yourself to either an artistic career or one where you care for others, you will do well. Avoid the hurly burly of finance, corporate life, and the ruthless cut and thrust of the trading world.

COMPATIBLE LOVE PARTNER - 372
COMPATIBLE BUSINESS PARTNER - 594

KNOWN NAME NUMBER

9 You can work alone, but you are much better off working in a team, where you have lots of support and help. You need to be around other people; when left alone, you tend to become extremely dreamy and unrealistic.

COMPATIBLE LOVE PARTNER - 373
COMPATIBLE BUSINESS PARTNER - 595

You can be belligerent at times—a typical characteristic of those with a Birth Number of 9—but you do your best to rein in this aspect of your personality. You also have a great deal going for you: you are a creative, imaginative soul. Others like having you around, as we know from your Full Name Number of 5, so long as you don't get too confrontational. Perhaps a clue to controlling your temper lies in your Known Name Number reading below.

BIRTH NUMBER 9
FULL NAME NUMBER 5

Extreme sports and dangerous activities attract you, Known Name Number 9, because they make you feel truly alive.

KNOWN NAME NUMBER

1 Although you have a reputation for being a leader, it isn't really accurate. You've never actually looked back over your shoulder to see if anyone is following. Look back now and you may see no one.

COMPATIBLE LOVE PARTNER - 384
COMPATIBLE BUSINESS PARTNER - 516

KNOWN NAME NUMBER

2 You are a very good listener, and any advice that you give is accepted as sound and practical. You have a unique talent for making new friends easily and readily, and you enjoy socializing.

COMPATIBLE LOVE PARTNER - 385
COMPATIBLE BUSINESS PARTNER - 517

KNOWN NAME NUMBER

3 You may well be a trail-blazer, a trendsetter, a pioneer—but a leader? No, not really. You may have people following you, but that's their business. You don't set out to lead anyone. You just go your own way.

COMPATIBLE LOVE PARTNER - 386
COMPATIBLE BUSINESS PARTNER - 518

KNOWN NAME NUMBER

4 You are very quick-thinking —an ideas person—and you have a lively brain that needs to be stimulated and challenged. You have the capacity for several careers in your life, and you rarely get stuck in a rut.

COMPATIBLE LOVE PARTNER - 387
COMPATIBLE BUSINESS PARTNER - 519

KNOWN NAME NUMBER

5 Earning money for its own sake doesn't interest you, but having enough of it to be able to purchase excitement and prestige does. You have an uncanny knack for making—and losing—a small fortune.

COMPATIBLE LOVE PARTNER - 388
COMPATIBLE BUSINESS PARTNER - 511

KNOWN NAME NUMBER

6 You have a very wide circle of friends and your taste in them is broad and varied. You make a great host and love entertaining, although there are times when you need to shut the door and see no one for a while.

COMPATIBLE LOVE PARTNER - 389
COMPATIBLE BUSINESS PARTNER - 512

KNOWN NAME NUMBER

7 Without a partner, you are poor indeed; it is only within the structure and intimacy of a relationship that you thrive and shine. It's as if you have to have someone to care about or all that energy is worthless.

COMPATIBLE LOVE PARTNER - 381
COMPATIBLE BUSINESS PARTNER - 513

KNOWN NAME NUMBER

8 Just wait a little while longer and the world will be ready to accept your ideas. Don't push. Don't argue. Carry on exactly as you are. You are right and you know it. It's just a question of time.

COMPATIBLE LOVE PARTNER - 382
COMPATIBLE BUSINESS PARTNER - 514

KNOWN NAME NUMBER

9 Niagara in a barrel holds no fear for you; nor does climbing mountains or canoeing the Amazon. You have more courage than is needed in this modern world. The planet Earth is just too tame for you.

COMPATIBLE LOVE PARTNER - 383
COMPATIBLE BUSINESS PARTNER - 515

BIRTH NUMBER

9
6

FULL NAME NUMBER

Always hanging around with the wild crowd, aren't you, Birth Number 9? You befriend all sorts of odd characters—these are the kinds of people that make you tick. To an outsider, you seem to prefer the company of your family—or at least this is what a Full Name Number of 6 reveals. Perhaps it's time to air some other aspects of your personality. Your Known Name Number reading below may show you which parts of yourself you should stop hiding.

KNOWN NAME NUMBER

1 You cannot fail to succeed, as you have more ideas in one day than we have in a lifetime. You will translate some of them into a successful business and will be very wealthy one day.

COMPATIBLE LOVE PARTNER - 394

COMPATIBLE BUSINESS PARTNER - 526

Bright ideas are always popping into your head, Known Name Numbers 1 and 5. Some might call you a genius.

KNOWN NAME NUMBER

2 By being as eccentric as you are, you only draw attention to the unconventional aspects of your ideas. If you were to blend in more, you would go much farther.

COMPATIBLE LOVE PARTNER - 395

COMPATIBLE BUSINESS PARTNER - 527

KNOWN NAME NUMBER

3 You are relentless in your pursuit of your dreams, and will continue planning and scheming long after others have given up. You are very resourceful and determined.

COMPATIBLE LOVE PARTNER - 396

COMPATIBLE BUSINESS PARTNER - 528

KNOWN NAME NUMBER

4 There is nothing you hate more than being bored, and so you keep yourself busy with new projects. You hate to be kept waiting for anything, and are capable of holding a grudge for a long time.

COMPATIBLE LOVE PARTNER - 397

COMPATIBLE BUSINESS PARTNER - 529

KNOWN NAME NUMBER

5 You are always at the forefront of a new initiative or project. You will do well in any occupation in which your innovative spirit is allowed to flourish, and badly in any field in which you feel stifled and bored.

COMPATIBLE LOVE PARTNER - 398

COMPATIBLE BUSINESS PARTNER - 521

KNOWN NAME NUMBER

6 You are very creative, with strong ideas that cry out for expression. You hate rules, discipline, and authority, and find it difficult to be supervised. If given the opportunity to run your own creative business, you will thrive.

COMPATIBLE LOVE PARTNER - 399

COMPATIBLE BUSINESS PARTNER - 522

KNOWN NAME NUMBER

7 It is important that you feel relaxed and comfortable at work, as your environment is very important to you. You are unconventional and need to work unsupervised. You can be trusted to do this.

COMPATIBLE LOVE PARTNER - 391

COMPATIBLE BUSINESS PARTNER - 523

KNOWN NAME NUMBER

8 You are able to hide your emotions well if you've been seriously hurt, and it takes you a long time to get over a failed relationship. You have a big, soft heart, and you deserve better than you've had.

COMPATIBLE LOVE PARTNER - 392

COMPATIBLE BUSINESS PARTNER - 524

KNOWN NAME NUMBER

9 Socializing is what life is all about for you, and you are usually the heart and soul of any party that you attend. You like to have a lot of people around you, but you never really take to them as much as they take to you.

COMPATIBLE LOVE PARTNER - 393

COMPATIBLE BUSINESS PARTNER - 525

You of the Birth Number 9 can be very complex creatures: expressive and poetic one minute, and then quarrelsome the next. Regardless of this duality, people are constantly seeking your opinion, as your Full Name Number 7 tells us. Your reputation as an intellectual always precedes you. But you are even more of an enigma than you initially appear. Your Known Name Number reading below provides another piece to the puzzle that is the real you.

BIRTH NUMBER 9
FULL NAME NUMBER 7

KNOWN NAME NUMBER

1 Nothing really sustains your interest for very long, and you may well need at least two jobs at any one time to keep you focused. You're not motivated by money, so it's no good offering you financial rewards at work.

COMPATIBLE LOVE PARTNER - 314
COMPATIBLE BUSINESS PARTNER - 536

KNOWN NAME NUMBER

2 You have an extraordinary talent for being in the right place at the right time, often by accident. Trust your instincts and you can't go wrong. You are extremely inventive, and can build just about anything.

COMPATIBLE LOVE PARTNER - 315
COMPATIBLE BUSINESS PARTNER - 537

KNOWN NAME NUMBER

3 As you have immense charm, it's probably best if you employ others rather than be an employee yourself. You work most effectively in the face of tight deadlines, panic situations, crises, and disasters.

COMPATIBLE LOVE PARTNER - 316
COMPATIBLE BUSINESS PARTNER - 538

KNOWN NAME NUMBER

4 You are one of life's great leaders, always in the thick of things, always the first to promote new ideas. Self-confidence is not a problem for you, and you find it easy to draw attention to yourself.

COMPATIBLE LOVE PARTNER - 317
COMPATIBLE BUSINESS PARTNER - 539

KNOWN NAME NUMBER

5 Your perception of your own importance makes you seem a little smug and overly confident at times, and this offends some people. Tone down your ego a bit and you will be better liked.

COMPATIBLE LOVE PARTNER - 318
COMPATIBLE BUSINESS PARTNER - 531

KNOWN NAME NUMBER

6 Nothing is more satisfying to you than closing a business deal. Being alone frightens you, and you constantly seek the company of friends. You are very reliable in a crisis.

COMPATIBLE LOVE PARTNER - 319
COMPATIBLE BUSINESS PARTNER - 532

KNOWN NAME NUMBER

7 You are a loving, creative person and are jealous of no one. You are slow to anger and tend not to jump to conclusions. You are very spiritual and well balanced, and are a kind person.

COMPATIBLE LOVE PARTNER - 311
COMPATIBLE BUSINESS PARTNER - 533

KNOWN NAME NUMBER

8 People gather around you constantly; but you tire of them quickly, and replace them as soon as they become predictable. Relaxation is difficult for you; you always have a project ongoing.

COMPATIBLE LOVE PARTNER - 312
COMPATIBLE BUSINESS PARTNER - 534

Your spiritual well-being is very important to you, Known Name Number 7, which is why you must take special care to avoid stressful situations.

KNOWN NAME NUMBER

9 You are easily bored, and love starting new, exciting undertakings. You hate to be kept waiting for anything, and consider tardiness a flagrant insult. You can be very quarrelsome when you are tired or restless.

COMPATIBLE LOVE PARTNER - 313
COMPATIBLE BUSINESS PARTNER - 535

BIRTH NUMBER

9
8

FULL NAME NUMBER

It is often difficult for people with the Birth Number 9 to find a mate. This difficulty stems from the fact that you can be, well, difficult. Much of your irascibility stems from the feeling that nobody really understands you. Others see you as unconventional, as we know from your Full Name Number of 8, and this might also scare potential partners away. Take a look at your Known Name Number below; it may give you a better understanding of yourself.

KNOWN NAME NUMBER

1 You don't just feel things, you experience them with every fiber of your being. When others are merely sad, you are totally distraught; when others are happy, you are elated.

COMPATIBLE LOVE PARTNER - 324
COMPATIBLE BUSINESS PARTNER - 546

KNOWN NAME NUMBER

2 You are intelligent and responsive. Because you feel things so intensely, you have a wealth of experience that others can only guess at. You are artistic and a bit enigmatic.

COMPATIBLE LOVE PARTNER - 325
COMPATIBLE BUSINESS PARTNER - 547

KNOWN NAME NUMBER

3 If you learn to control your passion, you can achieve success in whatever field you choose. If you don't, you will end up crazy and eccentric. You have great talent and an urgent need to express it.

COMPATIBLE LOVE PARTNER - 326
COMPATIBLE BUSINESS PARTNER - 548

KNOWN NAME NUMBER

4 Because you experience such powerful emotions, you can sometimes be a little rash in your choice of a partner. What you see, you instantly want. Learn to want what you need and not the other way around.

COMPATIBLE LOVE PARTNER - 327
COMPATIBLE BUSINESS PARTNER - 549

KNOWN NAME NUMBER

5 You set very high standards in your own life, which means you expect a certain order and harmony around you. What you dislike most is having that order upset. You are not very good at adapting to change.

COMPATIBLE LOVE PARTNER - 328
COMPATIBLE BUSINESS PARTNER - 541

KNOWN NAME NUMBER

6 You are a wild child, with great artistic expression and a real dislike of the humdrum. You also hate gossip, being bored, being bossed around, being corrected, being doubted, and, particularly, being teased.

COMPATIBLE LOVE PARTNER - 329
COMPATIBLE BUSINESS PARTNER - 542

KNOWN NAME NUMBER

7 You have great enthusiasm —sometimes a bit too much for the people around you— but at least you're never bored, depressed, or lacking in energy. You love sports and have a real competitive streak.

COMPATIBLE LOVE PARTNER - 321
COMPATIBLE BUSINESS PARTNER - 543

KNOWN NAME NUMBER

8 What a contrary soul you are. On the surface, you're calm and responsible, but underneath lurks passion and mischief. You can be extremely stubborn, even when you know you are wrong.

COMPATIBLE LOVE PARTNER - 322
COMPATIBLE BUSINESS PARTNER - 544

KNOWN NAME NUMBER

9 Outwardly, you are calm and organized, neat and professional. But underneath lurks a simmering cauldron of repressed passions and desires. Only your closest lovers will ever know the real you.

COMPATIBLE LOVE PARTNER - 323
COMPATIBLE BUSINESS PARTNER - 545

Your boundless energy needs an outlet, Known Name Number 7. You find sports to be very cathartic.

Both your Birth and Full Name Numbers are 9, which means that everyone recognizes you for the expressive, creative individual you are. They especially admire the way you stand up for the downtrodden. Danger and excitement attract you, and you are never dull to be around. But you don't always have to play the part of the quirky friend, you know. Your Known Name Number reading below illuminates other parts of your personality.

BIRTH NUMBER
9
9
FULL NAME NUMBER

KNOWN NAME NUMBER

1 You will get to the very top, but only because those around you are prepared to sacrifice it all for you. That is a great responsibility. I wonder if you take it as seriously as you should.

COMPATIBLE LOVE PARTNER - 334
COMPATIBLE BUSINESS PARTNER - 556

KNOWN NAME NUMBER

2 The big picture is always clear to you, and you delegate easily. You tend to farm out the most difficult parts of the work to others; but, then, what's wrong with that?

COMPATIBLE LOVE PARTNER - 335
COMPATIBLE BUSINESS PARTNER - 557

KNOWN NAME NUMBER

3 Trust you to get the job done, both within budget and on time. Listen to your heart a little more, and you may become more successful in your career. Dare to dream it—and then dare to do it.

COMPATIBLE LOVE PARTNER - 336
COMPATIBLE BUSINESS PARTNER - 558

KNOWN NAME NUMBER

4 You fool a lot of people who may think you a lightweight until they get to know you. Then they realize just how serious you can be. You hate being let down, but you recover fast. You dislike others seeing you upset.

COMPATIBLE LOVE PARTNER - 337
COMPATIBLE BUSINESS PARTNER - 559

KNOWN NAME NUMBER

5 You are a loner who enjoys solitude and your own company. And, yet, you are friendly and well liked by others. You are a little circumspect of love and relationships; but, then again, you can participate when you feel the need to do so.

COMPATIBLE LOVE PARTNER - 338
COMPATIBLE BUSINESS PARTNER - 551

KNOWN NAME NUMBER

6 You are one of the most unpredictable human beings around. Even this trait is unpredictable, as sometimes you behave with such normalcy that we are fooled into thinking that you've become one of us. What a tricky one you are.

COMPATIBLE LOVE PARTNER - 339
COMPATIBLE BUSINESS PARTNER - 552

It is when you are alone that you are most at peace with the world, Known Name Number 5.

KNOWN NAME NUMBER

7 Most people would describe you as eccentric. In the business world, this characteristic does not always inspire confidence. If you could manage to blend in a bit more, you would make more headway.

COMPATIBLE LOVE PARTNER - 331
COMPATIBLE BUSINESS PARTNER - 553

KNOWN NAME NUMBER

8 You are so determined to be right that it never enters your head to lie or to back off. You can be very pigheaded. Even with a gun to your head, you will never admit that you are wrong. And why should you?

COMPATIBLE LOVE PARTNER - 332
COMPATIBLE BUSINESS PARTNER - 554

KNOWN NAME NUMBER

9 What a mystery you are. You are a genuinely enigmatic person, full of wonder and secrets. You are a child of the universe and not a mortal at all. How did you get here? What are you doing here?

COMPATIBLE LOVE PARTNER - 333
COMPATIBLE BUSINESS PARTNER - 555

Famous People

CHAPTER 4

As we all know, the public personae of many well-known personalities can differ significantly from the way they are in private. Numerology allows us to see behind such façades, and to gain insight into the true personalities of these fascinating figures. Over the next few pages, we will look at the numerological readings of some of the most well-known personalities in the world. We have chosen only those people who have changed their birth names or have unusual nicknames, so you can see the numerological powers that can be unleashed by a change of name.

PRINCESS DIANA

BIRTH NUMBER 7

FULL NAME NUMBER 4

KNOWN NAME NUMBER 6, 4

Princess Diana was born on July 1, 1961. This gives her a Birth Number of 7, which tells us that she was innately spiritual, psychic, introverted, and intuitive. Her karma, or Life Path, was to discover the hidden spiritual side of herself. This quest was something she spent a lot of time pursuing: she had alternative therapists, three astrologers, spiritualists, a tarot card reader, an energy healer, a hypnotherapist, an "anger-release" therapist, osteopaths, chiropractors, reflexologists, aromatherapists, *shiatsu* and *tai chi chuan* experts, acupuncturists, and a mind-body therapist.

Her Full Name Number is a 4 (Diana Frances Spencer), with a 13 as a secondary number. The number 4 relates to rebelliousness and unconventionality, which could certainly describe her childhood and adolescence: after leaving school, she worked as a nanny, waitress, and cleaning woman before becoming a teacher in London—quite an atypical resume for an aristocrat. The number 4 also represents isolation, which may well describe the way she felt as a child of divorced parents. The number 13 as a secondary number is also very significant.

Nowadays, it represents magic and mystery, but traditionally it represented bad luck and disaster—even an untimely death.

When Diana Spencer married, she became known as Princess Diana—a Known Name Number of 6. The number 6 represents love and sensitivity toward others, which we know is an apt description of her from the abundance of charity work that she did. Many people also called her Princess Di, which is a Known Name Number of 8—rebellious, obstinate, intense, and difficult. This may have been a side of her that only those very close to her knew about.

And what of those who called her just Di? This is a Known Name Number of 4. As we have seen, the number 4 represents unconventionality, which her love life may certainly have been. Given that many of the candid photographs taken of her throughout her lifetime show her alone, we can also guess that she likely experienced feelings of isolation, another characteristic of the number 4.

MARILYN MONROE

BIRTH NUMBER 7

FULL NAME NUMBER 2

KNOWN NAME NUMBER 1

Marilyn Monroe was born on June 1, 1926. This gives her a Birth Number of 7, which tells us that her Life Path involved spiritual redemption, intuition, listening to her inner voice, and becoming a fulfilled person.

Her real name was Norma Jean Baker. This adds up to a Full Name Number of 2, with 11 as a secondary number. The number 2 relates to artistic talent and charm, while the number 11 relates to mystical awareness and spirituality. It is clear what sort of person Norma Jean Baker originally set out to be, and how she projected herself to others before she became famous.

It appears that her path was altered when she changed her name to Marilyn Monroe, making 1 her Known Name Number and 19 her secondary number. The number 1 is the number of the self, and of strength, drive, and ambition. The 19 as a secondary number, however, predicts disaster: it is the number of misfortune and self-destruction. Thus, here we have someone who originally set out to be charming, spiritual, and creative, but changed her name to become driven, ambitious, and, ultimately, the author of her own demise. It seems that while Norma Jean Baker's change of name might well have brought her fame and wealth as Marilyn Monroe, it also steered her away from her true Life Path and, quite possibly, toward self-destruction.

WILLIAM SHAKESPEARE

BIRTH NUMBER 7

FULL NAME NUMBER 7

KNOWN NAME NUMBER 4

The life of William Shakespeare has always been a great enigma, its details being largely unknown. Some scholars have even argued that someone else wrote the plays attributed to him. So what does numerology tell us about The Bard? His birth date is generally thought to have been April 23, 1564, which would give him a Birth Number of 7. Assuming that the 23rd is his correct birth date, he was born with a strong sense of intuition and was a very spiritual person.

His full name, William Shakespeare, is, again, subject to some doubt. There is evidence that the spelling of his name changed a number of times throughout his lifetime, from Shakspear to Shakespear and, finally, to the spelling with which we are familiar: Shakespeare. We shall use the last spelling for the purposes of our reading. William Shakespeare's Full Name Number is 7, and 16 is his secondary number. The number 7 tells us that others saw him as philosophical and intuitive, traits that are still attributed to him today. His secondary number, 16, is related to excessive confidence, a character trait that he is indeed thought to have possessed. Perhaps owning and

operating his own theater company by the time he was 28 helped in that regard. He was married at the youthful age of 18, and began producing children within the year. These are signs of confidence in so young a man.

His known name, The Bard, gives him a Known Name Number of 4. This tells us that he was full of humor and life—much like his works—but also unconventional and reclusive. His secondary number is 13, the number of magic and mystery. Mystery certainly did mark his life and legacy, from the question of who is the real author of his plays to the huge gap in our knowledge of his life, sometimes called the Lost Years. The Lost Years run from 1585, when his twin children Judith and Hamlet were born, to 1592, when he emerged in London as a successful theater impresario and playwright. What happened during these Lost Years? We may never know—there is simply no evidence of any kind.

Even Shakespeare's death is shrouded in mystery. Did he actually die on his own birthday, April 23, 1616, as some believe? Or did he die, as others have said, several days later? Is he buried at Stratford? Or is someone else lying in the grave attributed to him, as many have suggested? Indeed, the epitaph on his grave cautions against disturbing his bones. We may never know the answers to these mysteries. What we do know, however, is that even if he did not write a single word of the plays that so many believe are his, William Shakespeare will always be remembered as the world's greatest playwright.

NELSON MANDELA

BIRTH NUMBER 6

FULL NAME NUMBER 9

KNOWN NAME NUMBER 3

Nelson Mandela's real name is actually Rolihlahla Dalibhunga Mandela. The nickname Nelson was given to him on his first day at school. He was born on July 7, 1918, in a small village in the Transkei province on the eastern cape of South Africa. His Birth Number is 6. His Full Name Number is 9, with a secondary number of 18. His known name, Nelson Mandela, gives him a Known Name Number of 3, with 12 as a secondary number.

His innate characteristics are evident from his Birth Number of 6: he is idealistic, trustworthy, and has an air of martyrdom about him. His Full Name Number being a 9, he is seen by others as courageous and determined. With a secondary number of 18, the number of strength and achievement, one expects quite a formidable character.

His inner personality as reflected by his known name, Nelson Mandela, is a 3, which relates to energy, success, and independ-

Maria Sklodowska's Birth Number is 4, which tells us that she was reliable, trustworthy, and resolute. Her Full Name Number is 1, from which we know that others saw her as bright, honest, tenacious, and innovative. Her secondary number is 10, the number of attainment. From her Full Name and secondary numbers, we can deduce that she was the type that would stick to her guns, despite any threat to her personal safety. Indeed, this reading is quite accurate, as it was almost certainly the constant exposure to radiation during her research that caused her death from leukemia in 1934. She bravely continued this research despite knowing, probably better than anyone, the considerable risks involved.

Her known name, Marie Curie, gives her a Known Name Number of 3: energetic and hard-working, with the ability to overcome adversity. We know that she certainly was energetic, as her tireless commitment to her research showed. She also demonstrated the ability to overcome adversity, especially during the First World War, when she dared to visit the battle-fields in order to bring mobile X-rays to wounded servicemen. As a result of her hard work and tenacity, she was the first woman to win the Nobel Prize—let alone the first woman to win the prize for both physics and chemistry—and the first woman to teach at the Sorbonne.

ence; his secondary number of 12 represents completeness. His energetic, successful, and independent nature are evident at every stage of his life. He was born into a royal family; his great-grandfather was a Thembu king. Nelson's father died when Nelson was young, so he was raised in the king's household. He eventually graduated with a B.A. degree and joined a law firm. In 1951, he became president of the African National Congress. Soon thereafter he was charged with high treason. He was found not guilty, but fled South Africa nonetheless. Upon his return, he was imprisoned for twenty-seven years. After his release, he became president of South Africa. His remarkable energy and independence are indisputable, and his ultimate success in achieving his goals was complete.

MARIE CURIE

BIRTH NUMBER 4

FULL NAME NUMBER 1

KNOWN NAME NUMBER 3

Maria Sklodowska was born on November 7, 1867, in Warsaw, Poland. She changed her first name to Marie when she moved to Paris in 1891. She later married Pierre Curie, and became Marie Curie. She ultimately became famous for her research into radioactivity.

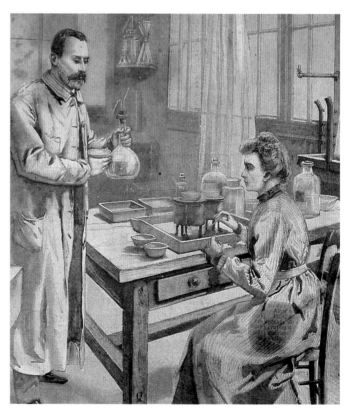

CASSIUS CLAY

BIRTH NUMBER 8

FULL NAME NUMBER 6

KNOWN NAME NUMBER 6

The man we know as Muhammad Ali was born Cassius Clay on January 18, 1942, which gives him a Birth Number of 8. According to this number, he is innately imaginative, successful, and intense. From his public persona and career, it is widely known that he is successful and intense, but imaginative? When one considers his poetry—"The man who has no imagination has no wings"—the introspective, philosophical side of his nature becomes apparent. His Full Name Number is a 6, which tells us that both his career and his outer personality are characterized by balance and perfection. When one considers his talent in the boxing ring and the gracefulness and skill with which he executed his moves, this reading rings true indeed. The number 6 also represents a gentle, soft-hearted nature.

His conversion to Islam led to the changing of his name to Muhammad Ali, a Known Name Number of 6 with a secondary number of 15. As we have just seen, 6 is the number of balance and perfection. The fact that his Full and Known Name Numbers are the same shows that others see him as he truly is: a master of timing, balance, and grace in the ring. From his secondary number of 15, we see that he can also be obstinate and reckless.

Index

Credits

Quarto would like to acknowledge and thank the following for supplying pictures reproduced in this book:

(key: l left, r right, c center, t top, b bottom)